Praise for M.A.C. FARRANT

"Farrant is a trapeze artist of the imagination, swinging over the existential void."—*BC Bookworld*

"Delightful and disturbing in all the best ways."
—Diane Schoemperlen, *Globe and Mail*

"A brave iconoclast."—*Publishers Weekly*

"Quixotically brilliant."—*January Magazine*

"One of our most original and imaginative writers."
—Margaret Gunning, *Edmonton Journal*

"A writer at the height of her creative and intellectual powers."
—*Malahat Review*

"A master of the Zen-like art of delivering
weight in a way that is featherlight."
—Bill Richardson

"M. A.C. Farrant is rapidly becoming a cult writer for her short fiction, written with perfect economy and with pungent and sometimes surreal irony laid on like thin coats of paint."
—George Fetherling, *New Brunswick Reader*

"Marion is too sophisticated for a schoolgirl."
—Miss Horel, home-ec teacher,
grade 11, Claremont Secondary

Also by M.A.C. FARRANT

Short Fiction

Altered Statements
*The Breakdown So Far**
*Darwin Alone in the Universe**
*The Days: Forecasts, Warnings, Advice**
*Down the Road to Eternity: New and Selected Fiction**
Girls around the House
*The Great Happiness: Stories and Comics**
Raw Material
Sick Pigeon
What's True, Darling
Word of Mouth
*The World Afloat: Miniatures**

Novel

*The Strange Truth about Us: A Novel of Absence**

Non-Fiction

My Turquoise Years
*One Good Thing: A Living Memoir**
The Secret Lives of Litterbugs and Other True Stories

Plays

My Turquoise Years
Rob's Guns & Ammo

*Available from Talonbooks

JIGSAW

A Puzzle in Ninety-Three Pieces

M.A.C. FARRANT

Talonbooks

Talonbooks
9259 Shaughnessy Street, Vancouver, British Columbia, Canada V6P 6R4
talonbooks.com

Talonbooks is located on xʷməθkʷəy̓əm, Sḵwx̱wú7mesh, and səlilwətaɬ Lands.

First printing: 2023

Typeset in Minion
Printed and bound in Canada on 100% post-consumer recycled paper

Interior and cover design by Typesmith
Cover print: *Adorable Cow* by Ethan Harper. ethanharperartprints.com
All photographs by M.A.C. Farrant unless otherwise noted
Interior line drawings by andrea bennett

Talonbooks acknowledges the financial support of the Canada Council for the Arts, the Government of Canada through the Canada Book Fund, and the Province of British Columbia through the British Columbia Arts Council and the Book Publishing Tax Credit.

Library and Archives Canada Cataloguing in Publication

Title: Jigsaw : a puzzle in ninety-three pieces / M.A.C. Farrant.
Names: Farrant, M. A. C. (Marion Alice Coburn), 1947- author.
Identifiers: Canadiana 20230461875 | ISBN 9781772015430 (softcover)
Subjects: LCGFT: Creative nonfiction.
Classification: LCC PS8561.A76 J54 2023 | DDC C814/.54—dc23

For Pauline Holdstock

The jigsaw ... is innocent. It is more innocent than poetry.

—MARGARET DRABBLE
The Pattern in the Carpet: A Personal History with Jigsaws (2009)

You must not ever stop being whimsical.

—MARY OLIVER
Upstream: Selected Essays (2016)

Prologue

The Start

My friends, Vicky and Patrick, understand the sedative value of jigsaw puzzles and that's why, at the start of the pandemic, they loaned me two from their large collection of Wentworth Wooden Puzzles. "Jigsaws will take your mind off case counts and variants," they told me. "They will keep you distracted, help stop you from stressing about the state of the world."

When she gave me the puzzles, Vicky emphasized that jigsaws are supposed to be a pleasure, an easy way to become focused. "I love working with the different colours and shapes," she said. "I love seeing a jigsaw puzzle come to life. I can spend a couple of happy hours working on one."

So, that is how it started. How jigsaw puzzles found me. I wasn't looking for them. But if a door opens, I always figure walk through it. You might end up in a closet, but you might also end up heading in a playful new direction, one you hadn't considered before.

1.

Whimsy Piece

According to Market Watch, the global value of jigsaw puzzle sales in 2019 was $689.2 billion US. For the same year, Ravensburger, a jigsaw marketer, states that twenty-one million jigsaw puzzles were sold worldwide. In North America that year, seven jigsaw puzzles were sold every minute.

This means that entire economies are kept afloat creating, producing, and distributing jigsaw puzzles and that thousands of people rely on the manufacture of jigsaw puzzles for their livelihoods.

There is definitely a surprise for me in those numbers.

2.

Puzzle States

TIME LOSS

Time loss is often associated with putting together a jigsaw puzzle. On the website The Mindful Word, Angelica Pajovic says this about the effect jigsaws have on her: "My perception of time, along with my ability to think of anything but the task at hand, is completely lost ... I'm living in the moment, and no external factors can distract me."

But can Pajovic's statement about losing the perception of time be true?

CALMING

Jigsaw puzzles can be a source of mental exercise and even comfort, as any puzzle enthusiast will tell you. They can also have as soothing an effect upon you as a glass of warm milk before bedtime, or taking half a milligram of sublingual Ativan at any time of day or night, as I will tell you.

Still, if the statistics are correct, twenty-one million puzzles sold worldwide in a single year means a lot of agitated people needed to calm themselves down.

CONTROL

Jigsaw puzzles are something we can control, unlike most of life, and most definitely unlike time. Upon completion, a jigsaw puzzle is a puzzle *solved*. When this happens, the feeling you experience is one of out-of-your-mind joy, as if you'd just won a big prize.

JOURNEY
Working on a jigsaw puzzle is like riding on a train; it's a single-track experience. Over and over, you are sorting through and then interlocking puzzle pieces, all the while loving or hating where you are in the process. But this can be an exciting thing to do because your journey has a destination – completion of the puzzle means you will have reached *the end*. Unlike your life, you know exactly where the end is.

LEAPING BEYOND THE RATIONAL
The word "puzzle" can be used as a metaphor, and this is useful because metaphors attempt to describe the unknown, the unanswerable, and the beautiful, and we want to understand these things. (Puzzle of Good and Evil. Of Staying Sane. Of Discord. Of Love. Of Why Are We Here? Of What Happens Next? Of What Do We Know? Where Will We Go?)

My mother-in-law Sara, for example, made a metaphor out of her dislike of birds.

"They're like imprisoned souls trying to get to Heaven," she said.

SPIRITUALITY
If there are books about the spirituality of puzzling, I have yet to find them. But these are the titles I would like to read:

> *The Power of Puzzles*
> *Zen and the Art of Jigsaw Puzzling*
> *Puzzles for Dummies*
> *The Puzzle Also Rises*
> *Jigsaw Your Way to Serenity*
> *Achieving the State of Jigsaw Flow in Ten Easy Steps*

The ultimate truth of jigsaw puzzles: despite appear-
ances, puzzling is not a solitary game; every move the
puzzler makes, the puzzle-maker has made before; every
piece the puzzler picks up, and picks up again, and
studies and strokes, every combination he [sic] tries,
every blunder and every insight, each hope and each
discouragement will have been designed, calculated,
and decided by the other.

This is what Georges Perec said about jigsaw puzzles at the start of his 1978 novel *Life A User's Manual*, a novel, incidentally, that adhered to the formal use of constraints as practised by the Oulipo group.

Following his thought, you could say that every book, every piece of art, is made by a puzzle-maker. Every sentence in a novel, line of a poem, brush stroke of a painting, note in a musical score, choreographed move in a dance is assembled so that each of us can experience something that is *designed, calculated, and decided by the other* to aid us in touching the ineffable.

3.

Regular Puzzle Pieces

Jigsaw puzzle pieces with heads, arms, legs, and indented sides belong to a class of common shapes called "Little Chaps," a term coined by Georges Perec in his aforementioned novel.

There is something innocent and merry about Little Chaps. You search them out in the heap of pieces, line them up, side by side, like a daisy chain, and experience great delight when you add another piece to the chain.

Alternate meanings of Little Chaps: little boys, urchins, penises. Note the lower space in the Little Chap is where the penis should be. Not to worry! Before long it arrives in the form of the Double-Cross piece, also dubbed by Perec the Patriarchal piece, the most common of jigsaw pieces.

Other puzzle pieces have names as well. They are, Perec notes, part of the Standardized Model of puzzle pieces, which sounds like something from Aldous Huxley's *Brave New World*, with its five types of engineered human beings – Alpha, Beta, and so on.

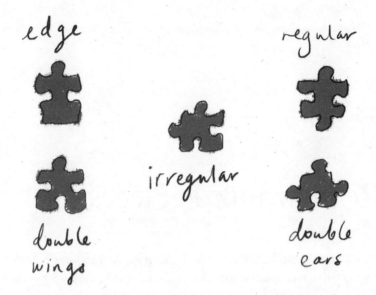

Likening your personality to the shape of a puzzle piece could be a fun pastime. Are you an edge type? A double wing? Regular? Irregular? There is bound to be an online game about this.

Of the Standardized Model group, I'm fond of the piece called double ears. My heart goes out to it. It's a bit of a misfit, odd-looking, perhaps misunderstood, but endearing with those double ears. It hears twice as much as anyone else and has a double soul, as well. Of this I am certain. It knows exactly where we go when we're "transported by music." Double ears hold a secret, even if the rest of us haven't got a clue.

4.

Puzzle for Brains

This is a picture of the jigsaw puzzle my husband Terry and I are currently working on: "Four Ducks and a Swan." The cardboard pieces are heaped on the old blue card table.

One of the puzzle's purposes is to aid us in passing time during these long winter evenings. Ordinarily, we'd be passing time by watching police procedurals on BritBox. We like the Detective Chief Inspectors, who have interesting flaws – OCD, politically incorrect behaviour, addiction to pain pills. Many are broody and loveless.

"Four Ducks and a Swan" has an important purpose, which has to do with our brains. We've been advised that watching police procedurals every night is bad for them because police procedurals weaken our brains, leaving them flat, dull, and devoid of imaginative content. Jigsaw puzzles eradicate this problem because they *enhance the brain's function.*

"Assembling and fitting the pieces together [is] a form of carpentry," says writer and jigsaw historian Margaret Drabble. "Using the glue of jigsaws, we are reframing our brains."

We would rather find a body in a ditch and piece together the mystery of how it got there, but never mind. For now, it is Drabble, Drabble, Drabble: Four Ducks and a Swan on a Pond.

So much depends upon the sawing and hammering in our desiccated brains.

5.

Whimsy Piece

Terry became a jigsaw dropout soon after we completed "Four Ducks and a Swan on a Pond."

"As fun and as innovative and awesome and absolutely mind-bending as a jigsaw puzzle can be," he said, "I don't find them beautiful. Once you've experienced the euphoria that comes with finishing a jigsaw, that's it. You know what it is. There's no mystery left. You can move on. I prefer imperfections and a certain lack of control ... I find that beautiful. I prefer any euphoria I might experience to occur randomly."

6.

Establishing Boundaries

I overheard a young guy in Canadian Tire telling his girlfriend, as they stood before the wall display of wrenches, hammers, and screwdrivers, "Eventually, I want all of these."

The girlfriend said nothing. Was she picturing their future carport filled with the tools still in their boxes as the years hammered by?

Yes, I thought. Say nothing. Perhaps it will pass.

She might follow the example of my second cousin Cheryl, who was able to nudge her future husband away from selling hardware at Capital Iron, which he seemed content to do forever – nudge him into becoming an accountant, one with his own firm specializing in commercial taxation.

But you must be strong in your vision, as was Cheryl. She knew what she wanted their life together to look like and it was one that didn't include wearing a grey apron every day or receiving a modest wage. What Cheryl had in mind was a smart business suit and a four-bedroom house on acreage.

Cheryl's husband, it turned out, was malleable and, luckily, Cheryl was coached by her grandmother.

"Get them at the start of the marriage when they don't have too many fresh ideas," said my aunt, the venerable Elsie. "Get an extra job to pay for the courses he must take. Put off having kids until he gets his certification. Then sit back, have your kids, and lap up the gravy. I'm telling you, life will be better for everyone if he isn't selling hardware."

Start with the edges. Then everything else will fall into place.

7.

Mount Fuji

There you are, applying yourself to completing a jigsaw puzzle. Your head is bent; you are absorbed by small, irregular shapes. You are separating the pieces – parts with human and animal shapes, ones with straight edges, different groupings of colour. All have a special place in the circle around the empty centre.

You narrow in. The picture on the box is your guide.

The puzzle's completion can take hours or days. Little by little you start seeing the shape of it all. It's like you're in an airplane flying overhead. You can see the general landscape of the puzzle but you can't see any detail yet. Eventually, details emerge – a yellow-and-white bird, a cracked vase. You keep returning to the puzzle, seeing new possibilities, marvelling at how you have missed the obvious. Godlike, you beckon to those around you, "Look, the sky is forming!"

When the puzzle is finished, you gaze at it in wonder. Perhaps you will apply shellac to its surface. Perhaps it will become the framed picture of Mount Fuji hanging on your living-room wall.

· This is what my aunt Maudie did. Mount Fuji hung over her chesterfield for fifty years. Her only child, Kenny, had bought the puzzle in Japan on his way home from the Korean War. It was a gift to his mother.

Working on a puzzle can be an act of devotion.

8.

Whimsy Piece

The etymology of puzzle – as a verb – is given by the OED *as "unknown," but it may originate from the Old English verb "puslian" meaning "to pick out," a derivation of the verb "to pose."*

A puzzle – as a noun – is defined by Wikipedia "as a game, problem, or toy that tests a person's ingenuity or knowledge." The solver of a puzzle "is expected to put pieces together ... in a logical way, in order to arrive at the correct or fun solution of the puzzle."

A puzzle – as a metaphor – can be a mystery, a secret, a conundrum, a riddle, an enigma.

9.

Infinity Puzzle

There is a class of jigsaw puzzles called infinity puzzles. The image frequently used is the Milky Way, the colours of the puzzle being blue, black, and mauve with white dots for the stars. Infinity puzzles give us an image with which to describe the cosmic mystery to ourselves. As a jigsaw puzzle, the stunning strangeness of the universe is something we can solve and put away.

But many of us see our own lives as one long infinity puzzle. I know I do. Because life at times seems to have no fixed shape, no starting point, no edges. It is always changing, always beginning, never completed, never solved.

Life can also be seen as one long sentence, as American poet Mary Ruefle notes in her book of essays, *Madness, Rack, and Honey: Collected Lectures*. She doesn't mean a prison sentence. She means the words we use to form the lifelong sentence that describes each of our lives to ourselves and to each other.

"That sentence," Ruefle says, "begins with your first words, toddling around the kitchen, and ends with your last words right before you step into the limousine, or in a nursing home, the night-duty attendant vaguely on hand."

We spend a good part of our lives tending to this run-on sentence. It takes a lot of effort. Every day there are countless stories to tell ourselves about what happened to us and why, and just as many imagined stories to worry over about what is coming next. Every day we are dominated by this ongoing narrative. It contains love, loss, ecstasy, moonlight, sunlight – all of it. It is both a galaxy and a single piece of a jigsaw puzzle, each piece eventually disappearing beyond the edges of the frame.

You can spend your entire life attending to this puzzle. Eventually, you get older and realize that, over time, you have been assembled and disassembled in thousands of different ways; all of them are right. You end up accepting everything.

The picture on a jigsaw puzzle box is your guide to solving the puzzle. In life, however, the guide is seldom as clear.

"It's all a movie anyway, the whole phantasmagoria ... There is no answer to any of it ultimately. It's just what is. There is only the moment," said actor Harry Dean Stanton, a person who knew what he was talking about.

10.

A Piece of Sue's Puzzle

This is a picture of a puzzle piece looking wan and harshly alone amid a quantity of dust and broken cardboard. It is a dark-brown piece and was recently rescued by my cousin Sue from a slashed-open vacuum bag. Besides the puzzle piece, she also removed cat hair, dirt, and needles from last year's Christmas tree. The scene presents as one of devastation and the aftermath of rescue – relief and solace. She had moved her dining-room table to vacuum the rug beneath it when the "mishap" occurred. Her husband Dave's current jigsaw – *Irises* by Van Gogh – lay across the table in pieces and when Sue heard a clunk while she vacuumed, she sucked in her breath.

Sue is another jigsaw dropout. "I enjoyed the Christmas puzzle in 2020 (one piece missing). I was over it in 2021 (two pieces missing)."

Annoyed by this pair of imperfect puzzles, she looked at the puzzle-maker's website to contact them about her "industrial sabotage suspicions." It came to nothing. She said, "Their contact page said do not 'contact them about missing pieces … nothing they can do about it.'"

The rescued piece, it turns out, was from her 2021 Christmas jigsaw of a train, and not the current puzzle on the dining-room table. Sue now blames the cat for hiding the piece.

The question remains, what will she do with the rescued piece? Return it to its box and its fellow pieces so that there will now be only one piece missing instead of two?

Sue always ends her emails to me with "Peace out," so I'm guessing it will be "piece out" from the vacuum bag and into the garbage.

11.

Notes on the Biscuit Puzzle

A jigsaw puzzle awaiting my attention has the image of a stomach full of intact biscuits as the picture on the box. The entire digestive tract is shown. I hesitate beginning. I make notes:

- A biscuit is a thin, flat, edible disk typically associated with the British. It is as stiff as an upper lip. You must suck on it to extract any flavour. Also described as flat, beige, round or square, a biscuit is first baked and then left to dry out and harden, sometimes for years.

- A cookie, on the other hand, is a biscuit that's become bloated, soft, though sometimes crunchy, as if it had lost control of its biscuit self and is now an embarrassment to its cousins.

- Mostly what we eat in Canada are cookies. Because of this, we are frequently seen as a somewhat spineless, though harmless, people.

- "Biscuit" is also the name of a flat piece of wood used to join two planks together. This is a technical description of the biscuit I was given as a child at my friend Rhonda's house.

As a treat, her mother would serve us milk that she'd dyed blue using food colouring. Early on, you learn unsettling things about people.

➕ "The crux of the biscuit," said Frank Zappa, "is: If it entertains you, fine ... If it doesn't, then blow it out your ass."
Even a seven-year-old can understand this sentiment.

♣ While there are hundreds of different kinds of cookies – a date square is a filled cookie – there are fewer versions of the standard British biscuit. A shortbread, perhaps an oatcake. Both, though, retain the signature quality of having to suck on them to retrieve their flavour, though usually there is no flavour. Teething biscuits offered to babies may count as a variation on the standard biscuit, but their value resides more in placating tears than in giving pleasure. Not everyone will agree with this statement.

♣ "Biscuit" was the *nom de plume* of the no-fun teenage counsellor at a United Church girl's camp I attended for a week in early summer when I was ten years old. It rained every day.
Biscuit's rival at the camp was the lively Cookie in the hut next to ours. We could hear her and her charges laughing like crazy after lights out, playing games, singing songs, while Biscuit lay on her cot reading romance novels by flashlight and yelling, "Just go to sleep, for Chrissake!"
The girls in our hut became lesser beings because of Biscuit.

🍵 There is a paint colour called Biscuit that you can choose for your living-room walls. The palette ranges from light beige to grey. According to the decorating-tip website Casa Omnia, "Biscuit colour is a very in-vogue colour lately; not only in terms of furniture but also in clothing and artistic trends in general."

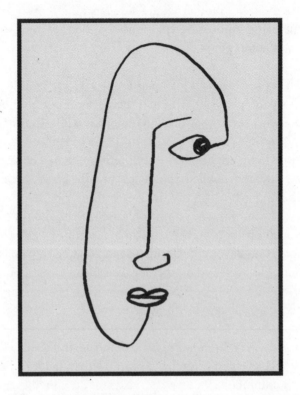

I'm supposing by "artistic trends in general" what's meant is artwork that's innocuous.

- Is there an "in-vogue" trend in biscuits? Yes, there is.

- In the UK, a popular biscuit, according to the website Joe, a news and entertainment site, is the Lotus Biscoff, a name surely derived from the food designer's yoga practice. The worst British biscuit is the Garibaldi, according to Joe, a biscuit that contains currents. Joe's assessment is one I agree with. "Currents have no place in society, let alone in our biscuits."

- Joe's very best biscuit is Fox's Chocolately. The ranking is accompanied by a fervid comment: "Oh absolutely Jesus suffering Christ yes!"

- On average, the British population eats eleven biscuits a week, mostly with tea. I haven't found similar data for the Canadian consumption of cookies, other than 303.71 million of them were devoured during the fifty-two weeks ending in June 2018. That works out to, what?

- Do all UK websites use "biscuits" instead of "cookies"?

- Cookie was a favoured name for cats and dogs when I was growing up. Now everyone is calling their dogs Cocoa. Which is something you can dunk a biscuit into, but never a cookie, because a cookie, true to form, will disintegrate.

- There are not a lot of biscuit crumbs left in a tin when it's emptied. Cookies, on the other hand, turn into crumbs at a shocking rate. The only good thing that can be said about biscuits is that they don't crumble.

- "It's a stark thought," said British writer Steven Hall, "that when we die, most of us will leave behind uneaten biscuits."

- A dog biscuit is a thick, hard noun used as a treat. Usually shaped like a bone.

- I spent a lot of time at camp in the nurse's station pretending to be sick. I didn't like Biscuit, or being pushed in the lake during free swim, or participating in group games like Capture the Flag because of the screaming. I did attend a session called Future Nurses, though. It was there I learned how to make up a hospital bed, should I ever wish to. The procedure involves folding a cover sheet in a precise way. The aim is to imprison the bedridden.

- The camp nurse was soothing Mrs. Arnold. She gave me a steady supply of Scotch mints while I was under her care. Scotch mints, unlike biscuits, are a pleasure to suck.

- Biscotti are not a pleasure to suck. These are the elongated biscuits of Italian origin coated with chocolate in North America to make them palatable.

  A North American biscotti is a cookie in hiding because, once wet, it will partially dissolve. But even though it is softened by dunking, you must still suck on it vigorously to retrieve any taste. As for eating biscotti dry, what is required is gnawing.

- Biscotti were used by Christopher Columbus on the ocean voyages to invade America. He needed a food source for his crew that could resist moisture and mould.

- It is currently chic to be seen in a café dunking a mould-free biscotti into an Americano while looking at your phone. This represents the high point of biscuit life in North America.

- In Scrabble, the word "biscuit" will get you eleven points. "Cookie," a superior twelve.

- I know of no Canadian child demanding a biscuit as a treat, nor of any adult offering them one.

- There is only one cookie that matters: chocolate chip. Specifically my aunt Maudie's, which she made using regular Hershey's milk chocolate chips and the recipe from the package. She added ground walnuts and used butter, not margarine as was stipulated, even though her live-at-home adult son, Kenny, would not eat butter, only margarine. No one knew why this was. Maudie baked her cookies in the oven of an oil stove. This may have been the secret as to why they were so delicious. They snapped when you bit into them but were soft inside. I could eat ten at one sitting. Kenny loved them, too. He didn't know they were made with butter. "Never tell him," Maudie warned the younger cousins.

✦ Sci-fi writer Neil Gaiman didn't appear to express any love for cookies when he wrote in *American Gods*, "The house smelled musty and damp, and a little sweet, as if it were haunted by the ghosts of long-dead cookies."

✦ For the record, long-dead cookies do not become ghosts; they become petrified crumbs. Leave a cookie tin unopened for several years and you will discover the truth of this statement. Crumbs remain on the crumpled wax paper or gathered like mouse droppings in the tin's rusty corners. Abandoned biscuits do not decompose, ever. They are waiting for your heirs to throw them out after your demise.

✦ The nurses' station was a separate hut and the only one in the entire camp that had heat. It was a peaceful place. The bed had a plaid cover, a side table, and two pillows. When I wasn't reading *Little Lulu* or *Archie* comics, I would stretch out and listen to the driving rain on the roof.

✦ On the day before coming home, I attended a mandatory craft session in which we had to make a biblical sentence out of alphabet macaroni and then glue it onto a round piece of shellacked wood. Our efforts were to be gifts for our parents when we returned home.

I chose the shortest sentence on the list we were given: "God is love." My project looked like a decorated biscuit.

My father, an "unbeliever" as he called himself, looked aghast when I gave it to him. What had he done by sending me to a church camp?

Nothing, other than providing me with a lifelong hatred of crafts.

- If you love crafts, you can purchase a cookie cutter in the shape of a jigsaw piece – the dominant "patriarchal" piece – and make your own biscuit puzzle with it. Once baked, the pieces are fitted together to form an ever-larger shape, and voila! A moment of delight envelopes your world!

- Biscuits are a form of roughage, possibly useful for moving the bowels, as demonstrated in the painting below, which is also the puzzle I have been making notes about. It has five hundred pieces and a name, "Biscuit Basket," which almost certainly refers to the contents of the stomach. Notice that

the biscuits are whole, a testimony to the fact that not even gastric juices can dissolve them.

I received the puzzle as a Christmas gift. It is now late spring and it is still in its box. Where to begin? With the sausage-coloured intestines? The esophagus? The pretty but odd pink-and-blue background? And I wonder, was "Biscuit Basket" originally meant to represent a vase on a table and, somehow, the image got away from the artist?

I have consulted my notes in order to reach a decision: Will completing this jigsaw puzzle of the human digestive tract featuring undigested biscuits add anything to my life? The answer continues to elude me.

12.

Not a Puzzle

I've just had a close look at the picture on our years-old cookie tin, which is called, with unintentional irony, "Finest Biscuits." Unintentional because our tin has always held cookies, not biscuits. Somewhere there may be a jigsaw puzzle of this image.

Notice that the tin has my last name printed on the top right of the lid. This is a testament to the tin's appearance on the bake tables of countless school fairs.

The thing that struck me about the picture, and what I had never noticed before, is that the younger woman on the right appears to be looking raptly at what is being revealed through the man's trousers. Her face is flushed! Is she embarrassed? Mortified? Aroused? But surely his trousers aren't what she's looking at. Mild erotica would not be appearing on a biscuit tin, would it?

Perhaps it's actually the man's right skate that she's seeing, or she's simply rosy-cheeked from the exertion of skating on a cold afternoon.

The subject of her gaze is the indulged heir of the manor. This much is obvious. A non-skater, helpless, soft, but a catch nonetheless.

The woman on the left is their chaperone, Cousin Mary. The man's name is Badger.

The younger woman is seventeen years old and an orphan with a potentially large inheritance.

Lucy Greystock of Mouse-in-a-Hole, Kent.

13.

Whimsy Piece

Jigsaw enthusiasts are called puzzlers. In earlier times – in the seventeenth, eighteenth, and nineteenth centuries, before the craze for jigsaws erupted in the early twentieth century – puzzlers were called dissectologists, a word that to our taste has unpleasant associations: forensic pathologists, the frog "experiment" in high-school science class.

The jigsaw puzzle was invented in England in 1766 by engraver and mapmaker John Spilsbury. His first puzzle was called a desiccated puzzle and was a map of the known world. His idea was to help teachers with their geography lessons.

Using a marquetry saw, later called a jig saw, which heralded the puzzle's future name, Spilsbury cut wooden shapes of each country. The whole could then be taken apart and put together again, and students would learn the names and placement of countries and enjoy themselves while fitting the desiccated map together. This is the map he used. Doesn't it look like a finished puzzle?

14.

Puzzle of Short-Term Memory Loss in Squirrels

We feed squirrels peanuts in the shell, leaving a quantity of them every day outside a downstairs window. These fortunate squirrels know where their next meal is coming from. One of them arrives every morning at breakfast and looks at us through the kitchen window. It wants feeding and I put out four peanuts. It's fun to watch the squirrel sit on its hind legs and hold the peanut in its paws and eat like a merry little person. It makes us want to take a picture of it and make the picture into a fridge magnet, or print the picture on a dishtowel and add a catchy phrase.

We've noticed, though, that many of the squirrels rush off with their peanut as soon as they get it and bury it in the lawn. It's spring now and we wondered why they'd be burying peanuts at this time of the year, because we thought they usually bury them in the fall for winter. Our back lawn is dotted with holes.

We think we've solved the puzzle.

Squirrels have short-term memory loss. They're born with it. This is an advantage for them and their food supply, because if they leave a nut buried too long it either sprouts or it rots. And since squirrels are hardwired to forget where they put their nuts, they keep reburying them. All through their lives they are burying and reburying the same peanuts and acorns and hazelnuts and whatever else they find to eat. This is how some of their food makes it through the winter. Like us, their lives are random and a little hysterical.

15.

Three Pieces

Upon the Queen's demise, a royal letter was sent to her heir, the Prince of Wales. In it were the Queen's last instructions to him:

> There are only three pieces to this puzzle. They are all you will ever need.
> 1. Never pass up an opportunity to relieve yourself.
> 2. Always sit down if you get the chance; it will save your feet.
> 3. If you must yell "Save me!," rest assured that a guard will appear with an axe.

The Queen further wrote,

> You, however, will not appear in this three-piece puzzle. When the clock strikes 10 a.m. tomorrow, you will be assigned to a new puzzle, a stockbroker's puzzle, say, or one featuring space travel. In any case, there will be nothing I can do for you. Goodbye.

16.

Tiny Heaven

There are many pieces of life to enjoy as we go about composing our one long sentence. Some of mine include watching children at play, walking anywhere, hearing music and choirs, reading certain poetry, watching murmurating swallows, visiting beaches and gardens, viewing that swaying tree over there, that drifting cloud.

Eating that piece of cake.

"There is nothing illusionary in this tiny heaven," Maira Kalman wrote in her extraordinary book *The Principles of Uncertainty*. She means a certain experience of life on earth, one that is anchored in the present moment. "I am silent with gratitude. I will go and bake a honey cake. And that's all."

Kalman, an artist, illustrated each page of her book with fantastic and whimsical paintings. They are irresistible. And the text is handwritten, so that together with the paintings, the reader feels invited in, as if to an afternoon party where everything is colourful and intimate.

Later in the book Kalman gives us her recipe for honey cake. Lots of eggs, dark honey, one and a half cups of strong, cold tea, half a cup of whisky ...

I say "she gives us" because that is the warm effect that Maira Kalman has on her readers – generosity. She is the champion of our sitting across a kitchen table from one another eating cake and chatting about how miserable and wonderful and funny the world is.

17.

Puzzle of Chicken Ears

I had never in my life considered that chickens have ears. But they do, one on either side of their heads. Vincent, the farmer I buy eggs from, told me this as a fun chicken fact.

"You have to push aside their feathers to see them," he said. "Their ear lobes are floppy and look much like our own."

Most of us wouldn't know about chickens having ears because what we usually see are dead chickens, ones without feathers or heads, chickens for roasting.

Vincent said, "Young chickens have light-coloured ears."

"And old chickens?" I asked. "What colour are their ears?"

"Black," he said. "As a mine shaft."

I swallowed some spit.

A puzzle is a deep mystery.

18.

Puzzle of Art

On a visit to the Royal Ontario Museum to view the Jean-Michel Basquiat paintings a few years ago, it was clear that we could not, by any stretch, afford to buy one. Nor could we afford the reproductions. What we could afford were the fridge magnet copies of the paintings for sale in the gift shop. But even those were expensive at $9.99 for one magnet, and you'd need at least six to mount a decent show on your fridge. Still, we bought six of them because we believe it's important to stay on point with regard to artistic expression. Fridge magnets are a big part of who we are as an art culture, after all.

Puzzle: *Every day there is tragedy; every day we make art.*

Clue: *A conundrum.*

"Art is a guarantee of sanity," said French American artist Louise Bourgeois. She reportedly hand-stitched these words in red onto her white bedspread when she was ninety-six years old. Her bedspread then looked like a tactile version of William Carlos Williams's much-repeated poem "The Red Wheelbarrow," and might be read like this:

> *so much depends*
> *upon*
> *the red letters*
> *stitched*

into the white
bedspread ...

But really, so much depends upon reaching the age of ninety-six. Bourgeois reportedly did her stitching as she neared this milestone. Perhaps it was done in answer to that tired question: *What is the secret of your longevity?* Perhaps, and better still, it was a final statement about her experience as an artist. I will sleep beneath this thought tonight.

19.

Whimsy Piece

At any given moment, on any given day, millions of bowed heads are seated at tables sorting through jigsaw pieces. What is this tremendous need people have to be working on a puzzle? What does this say about our global state of mind?

The bowed heads could be a sign of prayer, which is undoubtedly needed right now, given the state of the world, and perhaps working on a jigsaw puzzle is a kind of prayer, the activity being contemplative and exclusive, one that allows you to breathe peacefully as you handle the many pieces you are given.

Then again, the activity could be seen as a twenty-first-century version of the ostrich sticking its head in the sand. Another global zone out, like the addictive use of our phones in the face of catastrophic news. Or because of catastrophic news. Our phones providing us with a constant drip of fear and dismay with the idle scroll of a finger – "doomscrolling," as New Yorker cartoonist Ellis Rosen referred to it in a cartoon called "How to Stay Optimistic."

20.

Today's Puzzle: Road

This is a picture of the road we live on. I realize that photographing the surface of a road may be seen as an odd by-product of jigsaw contemplation, but notice how much the road cracks looks like a finished jigsaw puzzle. There are intriguing shapes, lines, and textures to admire. The slight colouration of the pieces set against the greyness of the uncracked portion of the road adds to the puzzle's interest.

Every road I walk along in my neighbourhood contains a puzzle like this one, usually several. These cracked sections are ready-made, existing unto themselves, waiting to be beheld, an unseen gallery beneath our feet, no assemblage required. They are reminders of the ephemeral. Once summer arrives, road crews will patch them over. Then the puzzles will remake themselves, perhaps at some other place along the road.

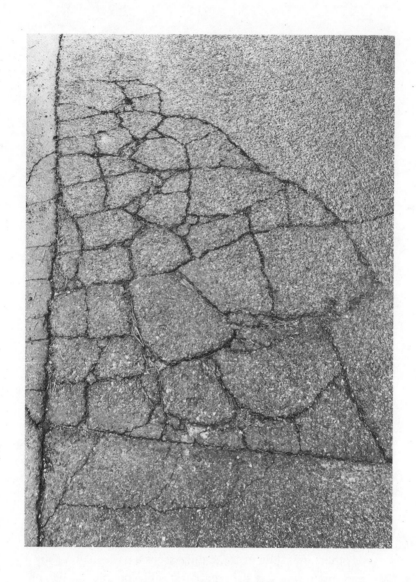

21.

Notes on the Great Puzzle

For most of us on earth, the universe remains in the category of "the mysterious unknown." I think we can agree on this. We consider it mostly at night when the jigsaw-blue of the sky is replaced by extreme blackness. Only starlight, lights from overhead jets, reflected city lights, Northern Lights, satellites, and the phases of the moon give definition to the blackness.

Occasionally, we experience a heightened appreciation for the vastness of the universe, as I have done on numerous occasions, often while ushering guests out of the house late at night, all of us standing in the driveway and staring up at the Milky Way, quiet before the whirling stars. Until one of us gasps, "Oh wow!" And we keep on staring.

Another piece of universe awe, I have heard, occurs while lying in a damp sleeping bag at night, inside a tent beside a lake, where there are too many mosquitoes now that the rain has stopped, and cracking sounds can be heard in the surrounding bushes, which could be bears or cougars after the garbage bag of food hanging from a nearby tree, or psychopathic teenagers out for a night of fun. In this case, universe-awe triumphs over panic. Hopefully.

For others, puzzling over the universe is a passionate hobby. I know a woman who says she is happiest while looking through her telescope and identifying planets and stars. She calls herself a star watcher and an amateur astronomer and told me her hobby is like birdwatching, only the quarry is farther out and more mysterious.

"You need stamina for being outside at night, sometimes all night," she told me. "You need warm clothes, a camp chair, and a couple of blankets. You need your phone playing Philip Glass's *The Hours* through your headphones to enhance the otherworldly mood, and maybe a joint or two to help you get into the rapture of things. You need a large thermos filled with strong Irish coffee. That's a must. And a good telescope, of course, and a tripod, and a journal for dating your sightings and noting any of your brilliant, far-out thoughts."

The universe without us is a factual construct ...

A galaxy consists of planets, stars, and solar systems. The universe is the infinite space in which galaxies occur. There are between one hundred to two hundred billion of them. Our galaxy, one of the billions, but cozily named the Milky Way, contains a mysterious substance known as "dark energy," which is still something of a mystery to scientists – what is it, how does it work? Even so, scientists assure us it pervades *everything*.

"Bummer," said my friend Gerald through a haze of cannabis smoke when he heard about this.

Then there is the fact that our "dark and quiet sky" is threatened by rogue meteors crashing to earth and space junk crashing into itself. Our contemplation is also threatened by light pollution from an increasing number of orbiting satellites.

We know these things because of TV shows, broadcast news, movies, and reports from professional astronomers. And because a recently formed group with the magnificent name of the IAU Centre for the Protection of the Dark and Quiet Sky from Satellite Constellation Interference has told us so. Made up of scientists, amateur astronomers, industry leaders, and Indigenous groups, its aim is to "protect the sanctity of the night sky," which is something most of us never dreamed was in need of protection. I will join the group.

About the universe *in general,* we know – we take it on faith –

that it's the "Final Frontier" of *Star Trek* and the eerie "beyond" of our homey space stations.

Furthermore, we understand that there are no other life forms in the universe, i.e., in infinite space. We also understand that unknown "others" might live there in some strange, unrecognizable form. Nobody on our planet knows which it is for sure, though speculation, curiosity, fantasy, and hope remain rife. We don't have all the pieces yet. What we do know is that you must float inside a metal capsule to get there, wherever "there" is, and that "there" goes on forever.

For biological life as we know it, we're told the universe beyond our planet is not a great place to be. This is something I've mentioned to my kids over the years: Don't go there! The outside air will kill you instantly. Actually, there is no outside air in space. If you are walking on the surface of your space station, either to repair something or for a well-deserved recreational break, you could become disconnected from the umbilical cord that provides your oxygen and connects you to your spaceship and float away like a puff of dandelion seeds into the cosmic vacuum cleaner.

All this, and the earth's many problems, too.

This is why finding planets in other galaxies is our one big hope. Because where else will we go when we are lost to earth?

So we spy on the universe, describe it, measure it, contemplate its black holes, send "probes," hypothesize about a Big Bang model, think about finding liveable planets *somewhere,* dream about colonization.

It strikes me that the notion of an ineffable universe is like Charles Simic's notion of great poetry: "A superb serenity in the face of chaos."

22.

With Reference to Cows

We believe that cows experience eternity by living in a perpetual now. Doing so, they achieve a kind of grace, an unintended cow satori.

And they are so unlike ourselves today, driving through rain to get the weekly eggs while worrying about Barbara. Will she invite us to her annual party, which is catered and includes live music and clowns on stilts? Or will we, once again, be left off the guest list?

We know it is remiss of us to dwell on Barbara and allow our well-being to be tied to her in this way. We know there is the whole of life to inhabit, one that includes people who are not Barbara, and also the "myriad things" that are rumoured to be out there – blades of grass, tree bark, small bugs, worms, clouds, and the like.

But if by some miracle we are invited to Barbara's party, I will wear my sequined dress and matching neon-red lipstick. You, your pink-and-yellow dancing shoes.

A puzzle about the difficulty of attaining cow satori.

23.

Puzzle of Chainsaw Yoga

I took a class in chainsaw yoga, which is supposed to be more calming than hot yoga, or corpse yoga, or the yoga you do at stoplights where you blank out and stop thinking, or goat yoga, which you do between rows of lavender plants while goats wander about, sometimes standing on your chest when you're in the corpse pose between the rows. There's a farm nearby that offers the service. I'd practised all these types of yoga and was ready for a new yoga challenge.

The chainsaw class was being taught by my neighbour Dan, a former tree faller, therefore an expert. His chainsaw was a state-of-the-art Husqvarna, a machine that's computerized and has a heated handle. We, his students, envied him. Our chainsaws were rusty, gas-powered, borrowed or rented.

To begin the class, we followed Dan onto a bare lot which had several small dead trees lining the perimeter. I think they were birch. Small dead trees are what you get in Dan's beginner class.

There were five of us, men and women, all past fifty. Like everyone else, I carried my chainsaw over my right shoulder. My hardhat was orange, my reflector vest yellow. I wore steel-toed boots – the proper attire.

There are three poses in chainsaw yoga. Learning the first pose, "Ignition," took up much of the hour-long class. There was an instructional film to watch on Dan's phone, a handout of a poem by Mary Oliver called "Don't Worry" to read, and a cover of Woody Guthrie's folk song "This Land Is Your Land" to listen to on You-Tube before we were allowed to ignite our machines and advance on the dead trees.

The second pose is called "Intent" and involves learning how to stride purposively towards destruction. This pose was the easiest to master.

The third pose, "Buzzed Out," is achieved when you cut down a dead tree. It's a pose filled with the buzzing focus of the practice but, beyond that, there is Dan's voice shouting at you above the roar, "Here we go! Here we go!" His voice and those words become like a mantra that stays with you for days, allowing you to maintain the sweet spot of yogic existence: steadiness, balance, and ease.

24.

Whimsy Piece

An extreme puzzler – someone who does several puzzles at one go – is, in some quarters, called a puzzle nerd, which is also the name of a Facebook page dedicated to jigsaw enthusiasts and an advertising byline for a seller of jigsaw puzzles.

I would suggest that "puzzle nerds" are single-minded, impassioned people and not nerd-like at all. The word, as defined by the Cambridge Dictionary, says a nerd is someone who is interested exclusively in one subject, is unusually smart, is socially backward, and lacks awareness of current fashion, a definition that seems outdated.

And it is unfair to apply the word to puzzlers, many of whom, I know for a fact, are good at parties and adept at practising the three phases of light conversation – the greeting, the talk, and the finish – and in remembering other people's birthdays and sending greetings and so on.

And there will be just as many exquisite dressers among puzzlers as those uninterested in what they wear, though many more puzzlers will reside in the happy middle of the fashion bell curve where sweatpants and T-shirts are the norm.

Puzzling is a harmless, well-intentioned hobby. Try calling bird watchers bird nerds. Quilt makers, quilt nerds. Fly fishers, trout nerds. See how far that gets you.

25.

The Merry View

There is a series of kitschy paintings called Celebrity Beasts by British artist Caroline Sykes that would make attractive jigsaw puzzles. Among the paintings are Ron Wood and Keith Richards of the Rolling Stones, whose photographed heads are superimposed on a double-headed sea monster; Prince Harry's head is overlaid on an orangutan; actor Helen Mirren's over a Siamese cat, curled and smiling beside her many awards, pink scarves hanging from the walls; actor Stephen Fry's head appears on a mighty stag basking in the light from four spotlights. The paintings are meant to mildly taunt the viewer by poking fun at our obsession with celebrity.

While assembling such a puzzle, you might experience a state of snarky delight. You'd be building up the image while simultaneously tearing it down through ridicule. You'd be touching on the absurd.

Or perhaps you don't love the absurd and prefer your "major" celebratory beasts to remain exalted. No blame there. Because what would life be like without our major celebrity beasts? The gods and goddesses inhabiting our films and streaming series, singing our songs, speaking to us as characters through books, guiding us from platforms on how to improve our lives? Where would we be without them? How would we know how to be?

This question qualifies as one to *puzzle out*.

I am more interested in minor celebrity beasts because I'm one of them, as is almost everyone else in the world, for good or ill. Read the obituaries. They're filled with cherished minor celebrities. Nearly everyone in an obituary is described as beloved, as the best person to have ever walked the earth, as kind and selfless, a joy to all, someone who was an incredible wit, who lit up a room when they entered it, someone who will be sorely missed. I always feel happy reading about these radiant people.

There are rare exceptions, of course, and these are the obituaries I collect. Not so much for the harm these lives may have caused others, more for the rest of us having the last word, the last laugh.

What to say about George?

> *Surely no one would accuse him of having been a loving son, brother, or father. He would have gladly stolen the shirt off your back ...*

Or Dave, whose obituary said he died suddenly:

> *His death was related to obesity, diabetes, alcoholism, inactivity, and a nearly sixty-year smoking habit. His doctor said he didn't know how he stayed alive for so long.*

Or Renay, whose obituary was written by her cheeky son, Andy:

> *She lied a lot. But on the plus side, Renay didn't cook, she didn't clean, and she was lousy with money, too. Hers was a bawdy, rowdy life lived large, broke, and loud. We thought Renay could not be killed. God knows, people tried.*

Or Jerry, who wrote his own obituary as a list of advice. For one last time, his family would have to hear his instructions:

If it isn't worth a plug nickel, get rid of it … Work at
a job where you get a pension. It will come in handy
… If you can't remember the truth, BS. If you can't
remember the BS, lie. And if you can't lie, you're not
much good, are you?

Minor celebrity beasts live among the major beasts as bit players in the human score. Some of the best ones are helpmates, role models, caretakers, sponsors of refugees, foster parents, hospice volunteers, health-care workers, eco-activists, involved parents, bakers of date squares for the community church sale.

Some are like the volunteer fireman who won a prize and had his picture in the local paper for being Best Volunteer Fireman. He was guest of honour at a dinner at the fire hall. Along with toast after standing toast and much clapping, he was given a wooden plaque with his name on it. He lives down the road.

Some are like Howie, who is also local and has a Facebook page called "What the Hell Just Happened." There is no question mark on the name of his site. It is a statement of fact. He knows what has happened and he's going to tell us about it. I am one of his forty-two thousand followers. Howie monitors the police band radio and posts and shares in his own words much of what he finds there. Alongside the homicides, house fires, robberies, and traffic accidents, we read about the inexplicable and the frankly merry. Howie is much admired for heralding the balanced view:

Lady at the Travelodge says they're putting snakes in
her drinks.
Old guy's taking hits from a bong while driving down
Douglas Street.
Two chickens on the loose at Prospect Lake.
Juvenile bear blocking Millstream Road.
Walmart alarms going off. No clue why.
Big guy breaks door of city transit bus, jumps off while
bus still moving.

Male walking in traffic screaming, "God is a hoax!"
Two ladies covered up in hoodies spray-painting graffiti
*   on a bank.*
Cig tossed from car. Fire on the way.
Kayak blows off truck!

26.

Whimsy Piece

The jigsaw world is an undemanding place requiring only the lowest level of fashion sense (pyjamas, sweats), decent eye-hand coordination, the ability to remember shapes, and the further ability to access neutral emotions, something that appeals to me more and more these days.

27.

Puzzle of Finland

In Finland – the world's "happiest country" for five years running according to a UN-sponsored index – July 27 of each year is designated as an official holiday and called Kippis. The word in English means "Cheers!" This is the day the Finns set aside for toasting everything good in life – and for keeping the drinks flowing.

Here is an example of a traditional toast that might be given to a couple married on Kippis:

> *Here's to your coffins*
> *May they be made of hundred-year-old oaks*
> *Which we shall plant tomorrow.*
> *May you both live as long as you want, and never*
>   *want as long as you live.*
> *May the best of your yesterdays be the worst of your*
>   *tomorrows.*
> *(to the bride) May I see you grey-haired*
> *And combing your grandchildren's hair.*

Kippis's alternate name could be National Jigsaw Puzzle Day because the day has so many separate parts. One of them is the tradition of throwing people who stay in bed too long into the sea. Since it's known that most late risers are artists, writers, teenagers, and politicians, a lot of irregular Finns will get wet on Kippis morning. Later, there'll be a community celebration where everyone gets drunk. Here, the main event is the annual wife-carrying contest. Finnish husbands gather in a field with their wives – or any person playing the role of "wife" – slung over their shoulders and form a starting line. When the gun pops, they're off! Dozens of husbands, many staggering, some collapsing from the weight of their wives before they reach the finish line.

If they do, Aabo Heikkinen and Seet Makinew will be waiting there with glasses of *salmiakki*, a vodka cocktail made with pepper, salt, and licorice.

Finland's midsummer celebration becomes a nighttime party in the middle of the day, an art form we can all relate to.

28.

Song

The power is out. The machines are mute. Night is falling on sideways rain.

This is where you find your ukulele from grade-five music class. It's in a box in the basement along with your school reports and yearbooks.

Huge gratitude for the flashlight!

Now you can sing about unrequited love in your cold, cold house.

A sorrow puzzle helped along by a ukulele and a flashlight.

And by the words of Beatle George Harrison about the ukulele: "You can't play it and not laugh!"

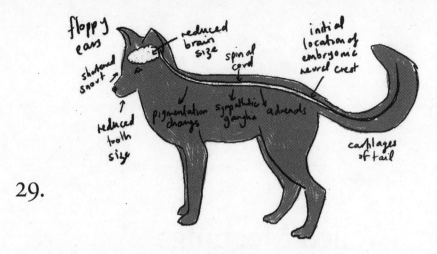

floppy ears

reduced brain size

spinal cord

initial location of embryonic neural crest

shortened snout

reduced tooth size

pigmentation change

sympathetic ganglia

adrenals

cartilages of tail

29.

F. Scott Fitzgerald's Song

Larger than a rat!
More faithful than a cat!
Dog! Dog! Dog!

This lyric is from a song written by F. Scott Fitzgerald and published by Edmund Wilson in his book, *The Twenties: From Notebooks and Diaries of the Period*, in which Wilson notes, "Dogs, for some reason I do not understand, always seemed to Scott somewhat comic."
     Another chorus of the same song:

Bolder than a mouse!
More wholesome than a louse!
Dog, Dog, Dog.

There is no mention in Wilson's book of what the tune for this song was, but I'm guessing it was light, fast and tinkly, created late at night after several highballs, everyone screaming with laughter. Maybe Gershwin was at the piano, maybe Zelda. Maybe Fitzgerald wrote the lyrics on the back of a cocktail napkin when he was floundering around for something to write after publishing *The Great Gatsby*.

30.

Veiled Meanings

A clue that often appears in crossword puzzles: *enigma with veiled meaning*. Answer (six letters) is always: *puzzle*.

The answer could also be *poetry*. Doesn't a poem seek to hint at what is hidden – insight, delight, the intransigent, the unknowable? A puzzle, particularly a jigsaw puzzle, reveals only itself.

What is not hidden in a jigsaw is its final form. That is, when the puzzle is assembled and its form is revealed. To no one's surprise, the image is identical to the one on the puzzle box.

But something that is not hidden is a puzzler's dismay over a missing piece. The right fingernail of Beethoven, say, or a portion of whisker on a cartoon cat. Look under the couch! Look in the garbage! Did the baby cart it off? Where the hell has it gone?

A missing piece means jigsaw failure. It's a reminder of the sloppy, chaotic world we live in, something we thought we'd kept at bay with our innocent, working-on-a-puzzle hearts.

About the hidden, poet Tony Hoagland wrote:

> *I don't know why I thought it was a good idea*
> *to go through life hidden.*
> *It must be something I picked up while traveling.*

Growing up, people in my family would laugh at anything – someone tripping over the dog or falling down the stairs, someone losing the aspic salad down the drain because they ran hot water over the container and it slipped out. Laughter, yes, but most in my family preferred to remain hidden. Hidden within their own tight group and keeping largely apart from the rest of the world. They travelled through life like a posse.

My aunt Maudie, a happy widow, always had a jigsaw puzzle on the go. It covered her dining-room table. As a visiting child I had to eat around the puzzle, careful not to drip jam on the boats travelling to the Dunkirk Evacuation during WW II, or on the small dog seated beside the beautiful woman, circa 1897.

Most people start a jigsaw puzzle by doing the border first. Maudie was a radical in this regard because she always began in the centre and worked towards the edges. "Otherwise, why bother," she'd laugh. "It would be boring."

She also said, "These puzzles are getting in the way of my doing nothing!"

I come from a long line of people sitting on the curb of things doing nothing much (while laughing about it), so Maudie's position on puzzles makes perfect sense to me.

31.

Whimsy Piece

Wentworth Wooden Jigsaw Puzzles are an elite line of jigsaw puzzles made in the United Kingdom. Unlike the lowly jigsaws made of cardboard, which is what most jigsaws are made of, Wentworth puzzles are made of wood, are hand-designed, and their designers are given credit.

Wentworth puzzles contain "whimsy" pieces as their signature feature. These pieces are singular and quirky and add delight to the puzzle's assembly by being "oddly shaped," that is, their shape deviates from the usual form of a jigsaw piece, but they're designed to reflect the overall theme of the puzzle. For example, whimsy pieces in a Wentworth puzzle of a snow scene might take the form of a sleigh, a Christmas tree, a star, a snowball, a pair of mittens, and so on, and would cleverly fit into the overall design.

Whimsy pieces, says the advertising copy for the Wentworth Christmas 2022 catalogue, are what makes their puzzles "irresistible."

32.

Today's Puzzle: Yellow Line

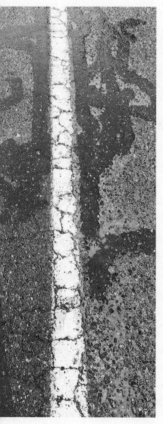

Here is another "found" road piece. It could be a picture of abstract art or a Japanese scroll or a jigsaw puzzle called "Yellow Dividing Line with Patched Cracks." As a puzzle, I could call it anything I like: "A Brave Glimpse at Existence" to get the philosophical juices flowing; "Road as It Is" as a prompt towards the mindful; "I Was the Real Thing Once" with a nod towards the ironic.

I am taken with the orderly line of cracking along the dividing line and what, alongside the line, appear to be brushstrokes effected by an unseen hand, but which are actually cracks, paved over. As before, the pebbly road surface anchors the composition.

This imaginary puzzle is an example of our penchant for making something out of nothing – here, a jigsaw puzzle is again created out of another random section of roadway. This is almost what Margaret Drabble says we do with jigsaw puzzles: "We are making something out of *almost* nothing."

33.

Whimsy Piece

January is International Puzzle Month and January 29 of each year has been designated as International Jigsaw Puzzle Day. The "day" was created in 2002 by American jigsaw-puzzle companies for marketing purposes – no surprise there. But with millions of jigsaw practitioners worldwide, it's easy to understand why the "day" has endured.

I'm guessing a person celebrates International Jigsaw Puzzle Day by doing one or more puzzles – nothing wild – just some sedate in-house puzzling. No champagne, dancing, robust singing, special foods, or invocations, though you might "dress up" for the occasion – wear a bright scarf, patterned socks. There is no mention in the various notifications about International Jigsaw Puzzle Day of having people over. But if you did, it would probably be for some silent group puzzling which, while sounding sketchy, is probably benign.

Though if you have ever worked on a jigsaw puzzle with another person, the experience can be fraught: "Don't mind me, but the piece goes there."

Fraught-ness is a given when doing a jigsaw with a partner: "Buzz off, those border pieces are mine." The puzzle fast becoming the scene of domestic carnage, resulting in one of you dropping out in disgust, while the other grimly continues with the puzzle well past bedtime.

34.

"Little Animals That Creep In and Out of a Room"

It took three months of steady work, but I never finished this puzzle. The little animals kept changing or disappearing or causing mayhem.

I would place the mouse wearing a red bow tie in the bottom left-hand corner, loving the way it clicked into place, but the next day, when I returned, the mouse had gone. Though not before chewing through everything nearby – the difficult beige linoleum-floor pieces, the tiny bag of white-rice pieces that took forever to place. It was the same with the ever-changing family of rats and their pink jelly-bean babies. Mess everywhere.

I don't recommend this puzzle. Or another in the series, "Little Animals That Creep In and Out of a Hotel."

With this puzzle you're always looking for the window-shade pieces so you can see if they've been left open. You're always hoping to catch a glimpse of someone having sex in one of the rooms.

Usually, the shades are closed. But one time they were open and I saw a guy in a white undershirt leaning out the window smoking a cigarette. He was looking straight at me.

Creepy.

35.

Puzzle of Dogs

In our town dogs are neutered or spayed, leashed, and trained. They wear fleece coats for cold weather, visit vets and groomers every four months, sleep on soft, round beds and eat grain-free kibble made of seventeen proteins, vitamins, and minerals. Their main activity is perching on the backs of couches where they watch the street for intruders. Usually, they only get to see children riding by on bikes and couples on walks. Our dogs howl for nothing.

Conversely, on the streets of Puerto Vallarta hairless dogs roam free in the neighbourhoods. When they're done for the day, they go home if they have one. Food is scraps, sleep is somewhere out of the way. Their world is other dogs – marking scents, procreating. If anyone thinks to ruffle their heads, they turn away. Like true philosophers, they keep their distance.

"A dog that has lost its coat is free from fleas," is one of their sayings.

"The prose poem is like a dog that thinks," is another.

36.

Puzzle of Meaning

"My life is one long story," said Penny. "It begins really sexy but then it gets sad and complicated."

She would be remembered as having accidentally brushed a famous novelist's sleeve as he strolled by her in 1982, thus raising the bar for living a meaningful life and accidentally solving the puzzle of meaning.

It happened during intermission at the Ice Capades. She was on her way to the washroom. Men skaters had just tossed women skaters into the air. The novelist was carrying a large bag of popcorn. His brown-leather sleeve brushed her right arm.

37.

Puzzle of Alice Who Is over One Hundred and Fifty-Eight Years Old

And keeps repeating the same question, *Who in the world am I?*
And keeps answering, *Ah, that's the great puzzle.*
Is she a living, breathing piece of paper?
A piece of celluloid?
An imaginary friend having an adventure?
An escaped figment of Lewis Carroll's imagination?
A living art form we feel profound to know?
Is she the Ponce de León of children's literature?
Has she found the fountain of youth?

38.

Favourite Puzzles

Daryl's favourite puzzle has only two seasons: fishing and curling. Half of his puzzle shows a runabout smashing across a choppy sea towards the horizon with Daryl in the stern grinning through the salt spray. The other half has a round black rock sliding across a sheet of frozen water towards an iced-over bullseye with Daryl on his knees holding an outstretched broom.

Daryl's is a duplex puzzle.

He has spent most of his married life doing this puzzle, seemingly to annoy Sharon, his wife of forty-three years.

What he hasn't realized is that Sharon is satisfied and happy doing her own favourite puzzle, one composed of a loving relationship with the TV set, dancing to anything by ABBA, and a willingness to never let a friend drink alone.

Sharon's favourite is not a duplex puzzle. It's a modest rancher puzzle with a vegetable plot out back.

39.

Today's Puzzle: Scales

Here is another puzzle I found on a cracked road. This one reminds me of scales on the backs of armadillos, snakes, or fish. Scales, which are composed of hardened skin or bone, provide the animals with protection from predators and the environment. The scales on a road (not to be confused with weigh scales embedded in a road to weigh heavy truck usage) are a sign of surface wear and tear. Without restoration, the road will break apart.

"Stop at the surface," Leonard Cohen wrote. "The surface is fine. / We don't need to go any deeper."

Becoming "arrested by the momentary nature of things within an unfathomable 'order'" is a good way to describe my reaction to the puzzles I keep finding on the surface of roads. The quote comes from *Backroads to Far Towns: Bashō's Travel Journal*, translated by Cid Corman and Kamaike Susumu, as does the following haiku by Matsuo Bashō (松尾 芭蕉) from the seventeenth century, which strikes me as the method of both assembly and disassembly of a jigsaw puzzle. It could also describe how road cracks come into being:

what was created
on the fan and prized apart
subsides together

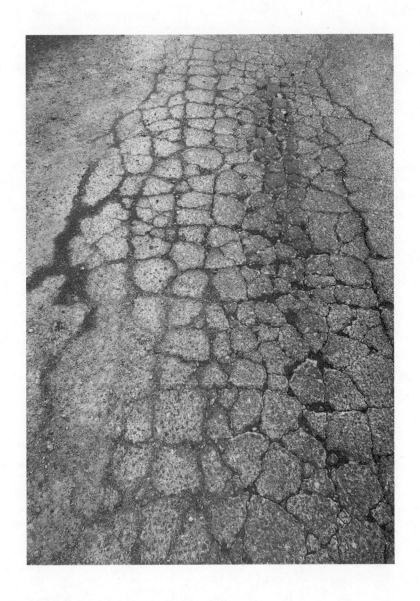

40.

A Day at the Beach

One of the Wentworth Wooden Puzzles that Vicky and Patrick loaned me at the start of the pandemic was called "Beer" (by Louise Braithwaite). The name was so at odds with the sunny scene pictured on the box that I renamed the puzzle "A Day at the Beach."

The puzzle's image shows many human figures scattered about the beach shore, huts with red-and-white awnings, sailboats, children flying kites, sea birds, and a vivid blue sky. The mood of this puzzle is bright, uplifting. But great personal happiness didn't make an appearance as I pieced it together, though a pleasant feeling of sustained warmth did. I smiled more often than I frowned.

This smiling, no doubt, was because of the whimsy pieces. They were in the shapes of an anchor, a treasure chest, a sea monster, a large strawberry ice cream cone, and, ironic for me, a clock with eight radiating spokes. Whimsy pieces are included, I suspect, to keep your spirits whimsical during the long haul towards puzzle completion. Shrieking glee often accompanies placing a whimsy piece, but the shrieks and the glee are short-lived and you are thankfully returned to the comfortable emotional state of flatline that the placing of regular puzzle pieces creates. This must be the rumoured state of jigsaw euphoria.

Generally, I enjoyed working on this puzzle and was amazed that I briefly lost time doing so. Amazed because I am a person who seldom loses time, a terrible flaw, I know. I don't need to wear a watch or consult my devices because I can tell you, often to the minute, what time it is. I've always regarded this quirk as a curse, the sign of a person who cannot be swept away, of someone who has a clock pressed to her heart. That "twelve-figured moon-skull, that white spider belly," as poet Mary Oliver put it.

A fixation on time may be my hopeless way of trying to control it, and Mary Oliver would agree. She called clocks "Twelve little bins in which to order disordered life."

But this state of things has also been called "keeping your wits about you," that is, knowing exactly where you are in time, and it's a quality that's prized as a defence mechanism against receiving unwanted surprises, good and bad. This "mechanism" means you are constantly alert and anticipating danger because you are focused on what nasty thing might happen next. It is being the rabbit, moments before the cat pounces.

41.

Puzzle of Managing Time

I will make an appointment.

Then my time will be well spent waiting for the appointment to arrive.

Another puzzle solved.

42.

Notes on the Desiccated Old Masters

There they are, the dear things. *Mona Lisa* in pieces on our kitchen table. Bruegel's *The Hunters in the Snow* unassembled on a sheet of plywood.

Would da Vinci and Bruegel have minded having their work turned into jigsaw puzzles? Or imagined that such a thing would one day exist? Could they have guessed that centuries later the outcome of their labour would be you and I assembling an 18 × 24-inch, five-hundred-piece copy of one of their paintings in order to pass our time doing an activity some might call frivolous?

Would they have thought this a strange thing to do?

And would they have minded their paintings being called "dear things," as in, the subjects of a peculiar jigsaw love?

Jigsaw puzzles continue to have a surprising effect on me. Besides causing me to see jigsaw puzzles in roads, they're also corrupting me with regard to fine art. I can no longer look at a painting without putting it into jigsaw format and wondering how easy or difficult it would be to assemble. I pay close attention to colour in this regard – how well defined, how muddy?

I thought Canadian Maud Lewis's paintings would make good jigsaw puzzles because she worked in the folk art tradition using primary colours. Her paintings are clear, bright, and exciting. Then I discovered her paintings have already made the jigsaw transformation. She's become a "Desiccated New Master" because many of her paintings, including *Covered Bridge in Winter*, *Family and Sled*, and *Three Black Cats* are now puzzles for sale online and elsewhere.

I don't know what this says about anything. Other than that assembling a Maud Lewis puzzle, or any of the Old Masters puzzles, might cause a person to imagine some of the excitement the artist felt while painting it.

There's an online site selling Old Masters jigsaw puzzles and promising "the chance to immerse yourself in the stories that these master artists weave in their paintings! The chance to witness their incredible skill and knowledge of light, form, shadows, and colour!"

There is nothing complicated about this pitch; all that is needed is a change of thinking. Buy one of their Old Masters puzzles and move beyond the usual calm application, perhaps even appreciation of the work of art, and enter a different mindset by abandoning your former way of seeing. This is akin to Tom Sawyer persuading his friends to whitewash his aunt's fence, a chore he hated. He did this by presenting whitewashing in a new light. "Does a boy get a chance to whitewash a fence every day?" Before long, his friends were giving him an apple, a kite, a dead rat "and a string to swing it with" to whitewash the fence for him.

So too with the Old Masters puzzles on this site. They use the same paintings that other sellers of jigsaw puzzles use, except that now, equipped with the tool of *new thinking*, we can imagine we are witnessing the moments the paintings were created. We can be story detectives, consider, for example, what is really going on in Hieronymus Bosch's *The Garden of Earthly Delights*. We had just never thought to look at things in this new way. Wonderment, the sellers are suggesting, will occur while we're assembling the Bosch puzzle; the mystery of the speckled turquoise bird with the woman's legs sticking out of the tulip on its head and the twelve naked men, some upside down, huddled in a circle around the bird's feet will be revealed to us.

Would assembling Desiccated Old Masters from this site, which is selling chemical-free expanded consciousness, cause puzzlers to arrive at the state of transcending self-consciousness, a principal appetite of the human soul, as Aldous Huxley put it in *The Doors of Perception*? Huxley, after all, is a "Literary Old Master" and probably a desiccated one, too, if his famous experiment with mescaline counts for anything, an experiment that caused him to pull apart and reassemble his own existence. If he'd spent time with a jigsaw puzzle after ingesting mescaline, his revelations might have been about the absurdity of trying to piece together anything – puzzles, a life. He'd be reporting on the sheer hilarity of the effort.

Huxley doesn't mention jigsaw puzzles in the account of his adventure, of course. His focus was on the astonishing existence of chair legs, the folds of his trousers, and the intricate construction of leaves, things he noted that were profoundly "nothing more, nothing less than what they were."

The next time I do a jigsaw puzzle containing roses, I'll think of Aldous Huxley and of this haiku by Masaoka Shiki (正岡 子規):

Roses:
The flowers are easy to paint,
The leaves difficult.

43.

Other Puzzles

"Crossword puzzles are excellent sedatives and should be administered to all, especially nerve-wracked cases," wrote Virginia Graham in her very funny book about "etiquette for ladies," *Say Please*, published in 1949. She listed a few instances in which a crossword puzzle might be called for – "nerve-wracked cases," those about to become brides, "those waiting for bad news, good news, or even THE news" – and praised them for their "drugging influence."

This "drugging influence" might have been at play in my father's case. While I was growing up, he had an up-at-all-hours job supervising the loading of lumber on the Vancouver docks and along the coast of the Pacific Northwest. There must have been a lot of pressure on him and perhaps crossword puzzles allowed him to "zone out" between ships. He didn't live with us, but visited whenever he could get away and, during these times, I'd often see him on the blue recliner at Aunt Elsie and Uncle Ernie's house where I was being raised, his socked feet tucked beneath him, lost in a crossword puzzle.

He had a low opinion of jigsaw puzzles and refused to do them. They required too much equipment, he said – an extra table, decent lighting, a magnifying glass, an abundance of time. He hated their continued presence in a room where, unattended, they could languish for months. He said that when a jigsaw puzzle started gathering dust it was time to hoist the white flag and return it to its box.

Crossword puzzles, on the other hand, were a tidy pursuit. All you needed was a pencil with an eraser, a crossword dictionary, and a cigarette burning at the ready on a side table. If you didn't finish the crossword from the daily paper, so what? Throw it in the garbage. There'd be another one tomorrow.

He would get annoyed with crosswords on occasion, though. In his opinion, the clues with obscure biblical references were created in anger by theologians.

"There they are in their miserable cells," he'd say, "living lives of privation and taking it out on the rest of us. Why couldn't they stick to orthodox clues, like the names of dances?"

When I was a kid, maybe eight or nine, he'd pull out his crossword dictionary, flip through the pages, and say to me, "Here's the clue, now tell me the answer. 'A ballroom dance originating in Buenos Aires, with marked rhythms and postures and abrupt pauses.'"

I knew the answer. It was a comedy routine we did. He'd asked the same several questions dozens of times.

"Tango!" I'd scream.

"Attagirl! Now guess this one. 'A fast rhythmic ballroom dance of Latin American origin with a basic pattern of two steps and a three-step shuffle.'"

"Cha-cha!"

"Now give me a sentence using the word."

"She cha-chas around town wearing gold lamé pyjamas!"

"Right again! Now take a bow. You've just won a million bucks."

44.

Cube

About Rubik's cubes, New York writer and wit Fran Lebowitz wrote:

> *You finish it. Now what?*
> *Congratulations, you have a slightly more attractive cube.*

Not a puzzlewit, our Fran.

45.

Twelve Down

Clues:

> One said the thing he said to every woman: "You scare me."
> One called drunk and asked if I still wrote crazy stories.
> One said his wife would be away for the summer and invited me to visit.
> One said parts of my body were odd and gave my nose, breasts, and eyes as examples.
> One said I was seductive because of the things I didn't do.
> One said I should cut my hair and wear long skirts in the French style.
> One said I looked better naked than with my clothes on.
> One said I was not quite beautiful.
> One said I was beautiful enough but should get my teeth fixed.
> One said he loved me but I read too many books.
> One said he loved the way I held a cigarette.
> One said I should try harder with his mother.

Answer: *Failed suitor.*

46.

Cross Words

1. Well along in the marriage he said, "Maybe I failed on purpose. Let me explain."

    The mung beans sat there rotting while she waited for his explanation.

    Example of a long-haul puzzle.

2. Because of your present mood, I picture you as dense cloud, threatening rain. You are like the picture on the box of my current jigsaw puzzle, "Grey Sky over Frozen Lake."

    Grey above, grey below, a razor slash of black across the middle. Harder to tackle than a puzzle of the moon.

    What will happen to this day? We're getting that kind of no-look chemistry going.

    Then I remember something from a book called *The Big Activity Book for Anxious People*, in which the authors suggests that no matter where you are, you can express yourself through art.

    So I do.

    I've added some heavy guitar riffs to the day and some dissonant harmonies, a thumping bassline and a posturing performance and called it the "Rockin' Blues."

"Lighten up, Baby. I'm in love with you."

3. "I am interested in having three orifices stuffed full of *patri-archal puzzle pieces*,"* the writer Maggie Nelson wrote in *Bluets*. "This is what makes me happy."

When they heard this, everyone who was working in the restaurant and everyone who was eating in the restaurant moved towards the steamed-up windows. Disturbed by the hard words of this unexpected puzzle, they pressed their foreheads against the windows and wept.

*See "Sources and Notes."

47.

Today's Puzzle: Path

There's a word for the study of roads: hodology. It's from the Greek word *hodos,* meaning "path." It's a geographical term, not to be confused with metaphors about pathways taken – or not taken – through life or with neurological pathways in the brain.

Rough or tended, a footpath is usually made of gravel or dirt.

What strikes me about paths is how much they beckon, particularly if a path is new to you. You are delighted, and a little fearful, to discover what's at the end of one, or around a bend.

The path in this picture is a straightforward and simple one, but it has its charms. Flat and wide open, it invites contemplation and unimpeded strolling. Grass and wetlands slope to the left, four willow bushes dot the way, and there is a faint outline of hills in the distance. It seems a solid and sensible path.

If you were the poet Bashō in the spring and summer of 1689 walking along the pathways of northern Japan "in sheer ecstasy under the beams of the moon," you might pause to write a haiku about the things you admired – an ancient shrine, a renowned waterfall, cherry blossoms.

Three hundred plus years later, you may be walking along a path like this one here, noticing only the blood pumping through your body, your easygoing breath, the air, soft or sharp on your face. You may be glad enough for this.

48.

Notes on Roads

How do you find your path?
In silence.
How do you practise silence?
By listening.

This poem by Ken McLeod from *Reflections on Silver River: Tokmé Zongpo's "Thirty-Seven Practices of a Bodhisattva"* alludes to the questions we have always asked of ourselves: Which path will I take through life? Can I choose more than one?

In the early twentieth century, Polish American gestalt therapist Kurt Lewin defined roads and pathways as "links keeping people together or distances that keep them apart."

In his essay "Sketch for a Theory of Emotions," Jean-Paul Sartre spoke of roads as "pathways of action, instrumental availabilities, closures, openings, potentialities, blockages, varying alternative routes" (paraphrased by Wikipedia).

Moving through space, then, concerns the routes we take, and some of these have been given names.

A route called Middle of the Road has its attractions for millions of people. On this road you follow the white or yellow line down the road's centre. You follow it surely and ceaselessly until you reach the end, where there is something like a brick wall or a bottomless pit or a stairway to heaven depending on what kind of person you have been in your life. You shuffle along the middle of the road with millions of others, often bored with the sameness of the route, but experiencing a sense of safety and togetherness nonetheless. Others around you may fall to the side, but you continue onwards, "toeing the line," one careful step at a time.

The end of the road is where you say your "last words." Imagine being so enlightened, not to say coherent, that you are able to compose a haiku on your deathbed, which is what Buddhist masters have done through the millennia, as in the following death poem by Dōgen (道元, 1200–1253):

> *Four and fifty years*
> *I've hung the sky with stars.*
> *Now I leap through –*
> *what shattering!*

Imagine being Aldous Huxley on *his* deathbed instructing his wife to bring him 10 cc of mescaline *pronto*! For the full "transitioning" experience.

The Golden Mean, also called the Golden Middle Way, is another road and tells us we must balance our lives between courage and cowardice; we won't get lost as long as we follow the maxim "nothing in excess." Lost from where? From "the straight and narrow," of course, because of recklessness.

Good things, the Mean says, come to those who stay in the felicitous centre between "deficiency" and "excess," as pictured below.

vice
deficiency   **virtue**   **vice**
                                                               excess

"The Way" of the Taoists is another option, but it takes years to figure out where this Way is. The only "road signs" are in the forms of books on the subject, like the Pāli Canon, the Theravāda, or come from cryptic poems, or teachers to guide you, or your own intuition.

"The Way," as I'm lately discovering, doesn't go anywhere. You "stay put" in the present, so technically it's not a road involving motion towards things in the future. It's a continual state of being in which you simply open your eyes and notice what is around you as you go about experiencing your life. Whatever arises is experienced deeply and, sometimes, with affection.

On the Road, the 1957 Beat novel by Jack Kerouac, implies a destination in the future, the start of a journey, and another novel of his, *The Dharma Bums*, combines youthful questing with the practice of Buddhism and so the future is discounted in favour of a zapped-up Zen-now.

There is a 1970 Canadian film called *Goin' Down the Road*, by Donald Shebib, that chronicles two young guys driving from Nova Scotia to Toronto, only to find poverty and disillusionment at the end of the road, the very things they were trying to escape, the message being that it's best not to have any expectations about what's at the end of the road because, technically speaking, we know what awaits us there. As Frank Zappa noted, "A true Zen saying: 'Nothing is what I want.'"

When the proverbial question was asked of me by my father when I turned eighteen – "Which road will you take?" – I said, "I'm going to be a writer."

Instantly, my father said, as if he had been harbouring a long-held fear about what I might say: "You will live a life of pain."

The thinking at the time was that girls should have "something to fall back on," a marketable skill (which writing wasn't) like typing, in case you're left alone after (when) your future husband has abandoned you for another woman because you were insufficient as a wife (didn't nail the tuna casserole recipe), or he unfairly died while the children were still young and you had no means of support other than to work in an office. Writing didn't count as a life jacket.

"Having something to fall back on will keep you from going on welfare," my father said.

I took his advice and worked as a social worker for a few years but had neither a husband nor children at the time. They came later, when I began writing in earnest.

49.

Whimsy Piece

Never attempt a puzzle that has over two hundred and fifty pieces unless you have put in the requisite ten thousand hours of puzzling labour and are now a Master Puzzler. You might want to keep this in mind. It will save you much frustration down the road.

50.

Puzzle of Lifesavers

It was the Thursday before Easter and I was well back in the bank lineup staring at the floor when the vision revealed itself to me. Others in the line were working their phones. For some reason I turned around and there he was, Jesus Christ, acting as a bank greeter.

He was passing around a plastic bowl filled with individually wrapped Life Saver candies. "Care for a Life Saver?" he asked, and everyone in the lineup looked at him in his dirty white robe and broken sandals, and said, "Um, no thanks." Who knew what was in those Life Savers?

There was nothing like celestial light happening in the bank that day because of his presence, just the blinking of the overhead florescent light tube. But everyone in the line had perked up and was staring at him. Expressions ranged from bemusement to pity to fear.

It was all over in a couple of minutes. Before anyone could say anything to him or have a mystical experience, he headed for the door, turned around, saluted us with the bowl of lifesavers, and said, "By the way, I'm not Jesus Christ, I'm Bunny."

Hearing this was visionary, tasteless, glamorous, perverse, crass, sexy, and confusing.

Did he mean for us to find him wrapped in pink foil beneath a rose bush on Easter Sunday morning? Did he mean for us to regard him as a hollow chocolate?

A mind-bending puzzle.

51.

Puzzle of Faith

The Dalai Lama was reported as having condemned Donald Trump. But his verbal statement, when we heard it, seemed cryptic. Or perhaps he was being balanced and wise. He was quoted as saying that Donald Trump lacks moral principles, but thanked Mike Pence for his support of the Tibetan people.

When you first hear a story like this, your heart skips a beat because it makes you puzzle, makes you wonder in whom to have faith anymore.

But then the writer David Shields's equalizing comment comes to mind: "We are all bozos on the bus. No one gets out of here alive."

Shields's quote offers perspective, but what I know is: Watch out. The road is in a hurry.

52.

Steps

This is what happens when you complete the twelfth step of this puzzle.

People will say to you, "Way to go!" "It's great to see you!" "You look terrific!" "Congratulations on everything!"

Meanwhile, the rest of us congregate at steps one through eleven, turning over thousands of puzzle pieces, searching for ones that fit.

Searching for something precious that cannot be named.

53.

Momentum

I saw a woman I know walking along the street. We stopped to say hello. I had last seen her a week before at the pet store. But since that time, she had aged badly. Like train-wreck bad.

"What happened?" I cried.

"Nothing much," she said. "Same old, same old."

Then she told me my husband was in a wheelchair, institutionalized.

"How can that be? I left him only this morning planting a cherry tree in the garden!"

"A lot can happen in a morning," she said.

A puzzle about moments evaporating in the heat we generate.

54.

With Reference to Cows 2

At their best.
Full sun. Ample grass. Together.
Same here.

55.

Puzzle of Fame

For most of us, not to love superstars would feel weird.

Not to share in the heartbreak and laughter that superstars provide would feel fatal.

This is because superstars are exceptional people. Much more exceptional than you or I, though we all want to be one. This wanting carries the emotional charge of hope.

This wanting allows us to arise, dissipate, shift, and move through our lives!

Because if you are a superstar your song will be heard at weddings. Your picture will garner love. Your obituary will last for days.

But take heart. Each of us can become a superstar, if only for a brief time. We too can become a spark in a galaxy of showering sparks regardless of who we are and whether we have talent. All we need is a phone, a stage set up in the living room, a couple of lights for projection.

This puzzle shows you how to get a poke at fame.

This puzzle is a reverie.

56.

Whimsy Piece

The excitement puzzlers experience over an unopened jigsaw box seems to be the same feeling one gets at the beginning of a vacation. There's the thrill of making plans for the trip (selecting the puzzle, then sorting the pieces from the heap on the table) and the great dollop of hope that you'll have a fantastic time while you're away (the happy hours passed as you complete the puzzle).

Jigsaw excitement evaporates, though, once you begin assembling the pieces, and calm focus takes over. This must be the real purpose of jigsaw puzzles. Working on one is like practising a form of zazen. Stilled at the jigsaw table, your heart rate drops, your mind empties. You try not to think about anything other than what is at hand, not even why you have chosen this pastime over, say, entering a sensory-deprivation tank, a form of therapy designed for the hyper-anxious that may "lead to clearer and more precise thinking" and a lessening of irritability and fatigue.

57.

Puzzle of Youth

This puzzle is about nature and fish and birds and oceans and whales and young people (and the music that goes with them). It's about guys wearing camouflage and driving jacked-up trucks with big mud tires while helped along by a heavy-metal soundtrack.

There's an assessable, energetic vibe to this busy puzzle. I don't know how else to describe it. It's validating, large and crazy. It's like reaching adulthood and becoming an action hero. You finally get to face adversity. Previously, you were always running away from it. Now you are facing that danger and driving through it. Now you are resilient, even when you're having a crappy day.

Now you have big visions. Like the English grad working as a barista. "I want to be like Gertrude Stein and have conversations with the world instead of just in my bedroom."

There are big dimensions, big colours to this puzzle.

The world is a magical smokescreen!

The "cherry pie is a miracle!"

58.

Puzzle of the Missing Note

- Does anyone know why the Royal Bank is closed? There's no note on the door, and trying to phone a bank is impossible.

- One of my housekeeping clients said it was due to COVID. Not 100 percent sure though.

- There was an exposure and they have to do a deep clean.

- It's ridiculous why SOMEONE can't put up a note on their door to explain why they're closed!

- Unless they don't have any staff to do that.

- That's very true and scary, especially since banking is deemed an essential service.

- There was a note in the newspaper. It said, "Bank Closed Saturday."

- The profit of the Royal Bank this year is sixteen billion dollars. I am certain there is some overpaid management person somewhere who could have got in their car and opened the branch or, at the very least, put a note on the door.

- EXACTLY! Their arrogance is amazing but, sadly, quite common.

- There was a notice in the paper.

- There was a note on the door but somebody took it down.

- Too bad they didn't put a note on the inside door.

- It WAS on the inside door but people using the ATMs go in and out. Someone ripped it off.

- There was a note put up by the manager on her day off, which someone took down.

- They seem to be having trouble putting on their pants.

- LOL.

- You'd understand that, sweetheart.

- Do you know when it was up, because I never saw it today or yesterday and it's really strange that it would not have been on the outside door?

- Someone said it was there. It said, "Bank Closed."

- When was this?

- Yesterday.

- There was no note.

- There WAS a note. I took it down.

- You f**k.

- Not okay, pal.

- You should leave a note where it's put up. Think of others.

59.

Puzzle of Mother

"I have caused complications among my offspring, who have become more like corkscrews bored into my head than servile children," says Mother.

A grown pair of them are crying foul about the embracing couple on the couch, meaning Mother and her boyfriend, Fred.

"This isn't it," say Jackie and Melba. "Only *our* lives are supposed to shine."

Is it because Jackie, once denied motorcycle lessons, now has intestinal problems? Is it because Melba, once denied a childhood trip to Disneyland, is now a threat to the security of every home?

No one suspects that Mother is more happy than sorry about this turn of events. Even with her usual singing off-key about her big lumbering Fred, Mother knows she is still the hottest gadget around.

What happens next is not revealed. But it will become immediately clear that nothing in this puzzle has been designed to placate anyone.

60.

Today's Puzzle: Lumps and Splotches

Today's road puzzle is a mess of lumps and splotches, a sign that little care has gone into patching the cracks. This has obviously been a rush job. My inclination is to scold someone.

But though the result of the patch job is imperfect and haphazard, it is not without beauty, reminding me that there is always a special quality to be found in a road puzzle, no matter what opinion I may have of it.

And I keep thinking about the young road worker who may have been responsible for the lumps and splotches.

It is late on a Friday afternoon, his friends are waiting for him in the pub, and there's this girl ...

61.

Dirt-Road Puzzle

Because I'd been noticing road surfaces and their potential as subjects of jigsaw puzzles, I was drawn to a series that is exclusively
images of roads. The one I chose to purchase is called "Dirt Road"
and is offered online at crazy4jigsaws.com. Others in the series
include "Farm Road," "Country Road," "Hilly Road," "Road through
Field," "Shady Road," "Camper on the Road," "Happy Trails," and
"Patriotic Road Trip."

I chose "Dirt Road" because the image and its title are straightforward, unlike the others on offer, which have cuteness or
nostalgia attached to them, an emotional appeal, or a suggested
narrative direction in their images. I like the fact that the image
used for "Dirt Road" is an unadorned, ordinary road, much like
the roads I walk along every day. I appreciate that such a puzzle
exists as a self-evident statement.

The photographic image on the jigsaw-puzzle box shows a
forward-looking dirt road with grass growing down the centre, a
forest of fir trees on either side, and a cloudy sky in the distance,
which is highlighted by a small patch of blue in the upper right-hand
corner. There are no wild animals standing about, no prettiness, no
colour other than shades of green, brown, and grey and a touch of
blue sky. You gravitate towards that blue like a ping of hope, which

is the scant emotional impact of this jigsaw. Overall, the image suggests authenticity.

Curious as to why a picture of an unalluring road would be offered as a jigsaw – it must be one out of ten on the scale for general jigsaw appeal – I wondered if there was a group of people who love plain roads and have an online group to share this love. They would naturally gravitate to a jigsaw puzzle called "Dirt Road," I thought.

The only connections I found in a search for "people loving roads," though, were of people loving to "hit the road" for travel and adventure, or for people wanting to love one another ASAP, which is a dating site.

"Dirt Road" has one thousand cardboard pieces, all of them small. Before opening the box, I wondered if the puzzle would be difficult or boring to assemble. I soon discovered it was both.

Naturally, I tackled the blue-sky portion of "Dirt Road" first. There were only eleven blue pieces and I thought this part would be the easiest to begin with, because the nine hundred and eighty-nine other pieces were making me feel queasy. I worked at the puzzle for thirty-five minutes, managing to place only two blue pieces. This is when I discovered that I was bored; I was experiencing a solid, mind-dulling form of weariness. I felt I wasn't the right person to solve the "Dirt Road" puzzle that day and walked away from it.

I returned to the puzzle a few days later and managed to place a few of the dirt pieces. This absorbed me for a while. When I finished there was a small brown splotch on the table.

Avoiding the recurring boredom this puzzle caused became a full-time activity. And besides the boredom I experienced, I was disappointed. I had thought my remarks about the high worth – the authenticity – of the puzzle's image would sustain me through the assembly.

I am optimistic that my mood will change, but so far, the hangover from this particular jigsaw puzzle is lasting.

62.

Notes on Boredom

I came across a line of boring jigsaw puzzles. Or more precisely, they were puzzles that have, as their advertised subject, the state of boredom. The images and titles included "Ottawa Is Boring" (Parliament buildings); "Bored Cat with Glasses" (obvious); "Hell Was Boring" (white medieval script on red background); "Normal Is Boring" (cross-eyed happy face with protruding blood-red tongue); "S.O.S. I'm Boring" (sinking ship).

Writer David Foster Wallace called boredom the "terror of silence with nothing diverting to do." Philosopher Jean Baudrillard described it as "a pitiless zooming in on the epidermis of time. Every instant is dilated and magnified like the pores of the face."

And poet Joseph Brodsky, 1987 Nobel Laureate in Literature, told graduating students in a commencement address at Dartmouth College in 1995: "When hit by boredom, let yourself be crushed by it; submerge, hit bottom ... The reason boredom deserves such scrutiny is that it represents pure, undiluted time in all its repetitive, redundant, monotonous splendour." He also advised the students to get used to boredom because boredom was going to take up much of their lives.

I discovered there are five types of boredom, according to a 2013 article published on the website Mental Floss: apathetic, reactant, searching, calibrating, and indifferent. The fifth one – "indifferent" – is defined as "feeling relaxed and fatigued but cheerful," which doesn't sound so bad. It means lying on the bed on a weekday afternoon and reading a science-fiction novel about lust in another galaxy. Or gazing out the window at heavy grey clouds while listening to a funereal piece of music by Arvo Pärt.

"Calibrating boredom," according to the definition, is feeling bored and feeling vague about doing something about it.

"Searching boredom" is being fed up with being bored and represents the slow climb out of the pit in search of something to do, usually a walk, a hobby, or a jigsaw puzzle.

Some people claim they are never bored. Time isn't "heavy on their hands" because there isn't enough time in a day to stare out a window. They're not waiting for something to happen ("reactive boredom") because, between work and children and household chores, everything is happening. What they wish for is time away and alone.

My mother-in-law Sara said she was never bored. She considered this to be an admirable quality. She lived with us in a downstairs suite for seventeen years, so I was able to observe her lack of boredom at close range. And it's true, I never once caught her brooding over the hard questions, or fleeing from the silence of a room. There *was* no silence, no stagnant time. Travel, family, and the game of bridge, which involved a lot of back-and-forth parties, kept her *too busy* to be bored.

My aunt Elsie was the same. Sewing, knitting, "keeping house," buying groceries, shoving marigolds into the dreary strip of garden beside our house, shoving her fingers into every family member's flesh – these things kept her busy. Busyness was her corrective against boredom and morbidity.

"Don't be so bloody morbid," she'd say when I was a teenager and mentioned death or the meaninglessness of life (I'd just discovered Camus). She worried something was wrong with me because I pondered such questions. Worried that I'd become "too deep" for any man to want, that I'd become boring, and a boring woman was "beyond the pale."

Women, I thought she believed, should be like the woman in the "Good Wife Guide" illustration from *Housekeeping Monthly*, dated May 13, 1955. Elsie had cut it out and kept it in the tea-towel drawer, which was baffling to me. Bossy and tough, she was nothing like the picture of the young blond woman who serves as the article's example. This woman wears a ruffled apron and is seen presenting a roast beef on a platter, while smiling ecstatically to no one in particular.

She is ecstatic, I suppose, because she's solved the puzzle of what it takes to make a good wife. Some of the pieces needed to complete this puzzle are noted as bullet points in the illustration: "Arrange his pillow!" "Take off his shoes!" "Know your place!" "Be a little gay [*sic*]!" "Touch up your makeup!" "Remember, his boring day may need a lift and it's one of your duties in life to provide it!"

The saved illustration, I'm now certain, was Elsie's idea of a joke. Because doing any of these things, especially kneeling before Ernie to take off his shoes, or "knowing her place," that is, under his foot, would have left her rolling on the floor in laughter.

63.

Puzzle of Palm Springs

There is a life-sized bronze statue of deceased pop star Sonny Bono standing in front of his former restaurant on Palm Canyon Drive. The living Leonardo DiCaprio is glimpsed sitting sideways at a bar two doors down. And Barack Obama and his family are arriving any moment by private jet for a well-deserved holiday, or so we have heard.

Have they read the same brochures we have? The ones advertising tours of cactus gardens and reptile zoos? Tram rides across drought-stricken hills?

Will they, when they're driving in their armoured vehicle to wherever they're staying, catch sight of the turquoise-and-pink billboard with the happy couple urging visitors to play non-stop in this "desert paradise"?

Like us, the Obamas are bound to see the nude riding his bike along the main drag every day at five to mark the hour like a striking clock. Or if they're walking about disguised as tourists – sunglasses, flip-flops, eating complimentary gelato out of tiny paper cups – they might be offered free drink tickets outside Toucans Tiki Lounge from a man dressed as Spider-Man. If it's a Sunday, they can drink endless margaritas at the Bitchiest Brunch at Oscar's while watching the outdoor show *Diamonds Are a Girl's Best Friend*!

Do the Obamas know that drag queens are beautiful and can be seven feet tall?

And will the Obamas notice that, despite the years-long drought, the town's seventeen golf courses are kept green with trucked-in water? And that beside every bougainvillea-covered gate in the wealthy neighbourhoods are signs that read *Keep Out! Armed Response!*

Will they know about the curtain, the one we parted to reveal the Palm Springs underclass? The Mexican workers making deliveries, fixing faulty swimming-pool filters at dawn, sweeping the Walk of Stars at midnight, men and women providing their services invisibly, like phantoms.

And will they notice the beggars, the scruffy kids with their packs and unkempt hair, who walk swiftly along the streets? They're not allowed to sit on the curbs, benches, or grass; there's a town ordinance against it.

The kids look almost healthy compared to the puffy tourists from Canada and the US Midwest with their pale winter skin. Like us, they're wearing last summer's shorts and sandals, carrying saved-up money in pouches around their waists.

Rumour has it the beggars are really method actors from LA hired by the town to give depth to our experience of unhinged wealth, so that encountering a beggar will make us feel our privilege even more and thus impel us to shop and drink with impunity.

In Palm Springs, trying to fit all the pieces of this world together gets mixed reviews.

64.

Puzzle of Independence

This puzzle's image is a closeup of crumbly dirt with sections of worms and weeds interspersed throughout, mostly done in shades of brown. It's a puzzle that only the most dedicated puzzler can complete and it leads me to the realization that instead of staring with a drooping mouth at the pile of pieces on the table, I can refuse this task and leave it unfinished. In fact, there are many puzzles in the world that I can do this to or that I will never even see.

Why struggle over someone else's puzzle when I can create my own, one that includes birds with pink feathers, and a new variety of cat called a Lace Cat that has haunches made of lace? Or one that has a goat leaping through a prismatic arch while a chameleon bird changes from red to green to orange like an out-of-control stoplight?

All my puzzles will have dreamtime figures wandering about in them. The reason for their existence may be unclear, but the reason is nevertheless important.

65.

Darkness

There is nothing to relieve the darkness of this puzzle. No star, no shadow, no moonlight. No faint outline of lovers hurrying to a hayloft beyond the frame.

The box description says, "It is totally night. The wild era of joy has ended." It quotes Saint-Exupéry's *The Little Prince*: "You are beautiful, but you are empty."

Each piece of this puzzle is the same ink-black colour, the same size and shape.

Look! You can almost see the graveyard from here!

66.

Jigsaw Death

Is there such a thing as Jigsaw Death?

How many people have dropped dead while doing a jigsaw puzzle? Their heads slumped on the table, pieces scattered on the floor, the tricky bit of an angel's halo having suddenly gone askew, the dead person's fist clutching the crucial corner piece of the stained-glass nativity scene, the cat sniffing about the body, dinner spoiling in the oven, the sun about to set, finally and forever.

Are there any statistics for this?

Could Jigsaw Death become a subcategory in the forensic sciences? Could it figure in detective novels? Did Agatha Christie miss the boat by not writing a mystery with the title "Death by Jigsaw Puzzle"?

Could a copycat death occur, say while working on the puzzle called "The Death of Socrates," a five-hundred-piece puzzle made from the 1787 painting by Jacques-Louis David which shows Socrates holding forth before his weeping followers while reaching for the cup of hemlock? If you were a philosophical sort of person and identified with Socrates, there might be something fitting about this end for you.

Or could Puzzle Death occur because a puzzler didn't heed the warning on the box it came in – "Choking hazard. Small parts.

Not for children under three" – and chewed on a puzzle piece, accidentally swallowed it, and then choked to death?

The Heimlich manoeuvre, also known as "abdominal thrusts," was invented by American surgeon and researcher Henry Heimlich in the mid-twentieth century. It has saved many people from death by choking, possibly puzzlers among them.

My sole function as a parent, as I saw it, was to keep my children alive. While they were growing up, I'd often say to them, "I hope you're getting this down," because I'd be imparting important pieces of advice to them, such as: Don't have a raccoon for a pet; they can turn nasty and tear your face off. Don't do drugs and then wander through a forest at night because you could get lost and die. Don't row across a large body of water when you're drunk because you won't be paying attention to waves or floating logs and the boat could tip and you could drown and die. Don't mix bleach and ammonia to use as a cleaning product because the fumes will kill you. Don't text on your phone while walking across a city street because a bus could hit you or a person could fall out of the twenty-fourth-storey window of a building and land on you, or you could walk into a building, knock yourself out, and die.

I insisted they learn the Heimlich manoeuvre. Why? Because life is more comfortable if you are not choking on a piece of something or other.

I said, and they will verify this, "The Heimlich manoeuvre is basic first aid and a skill you must have. So that when a person in your company starts choking on a piece of food you can save them from certain death. That way you won't be struck with speechless horror as the person's life extinguishes before your eyes; you won't carry this vision around with you for the rest of your lives. I know what I'm talking about. I watched a film on the subject at school when I was eight years old and it has terrorized me all my life. The film showed a father trying to save a girl my age by puncturing her throat – he had a knife in his hand – so she could breathe because she was choking on a piece of meat. A doctor intervened just at that crucial moment – he'd apparently been hiding behind the floor-length brocade curtains in the living room just waiting for this crisis – and taught the family the Heimlich manoeuvre. The girl lived. I rest my case."

But I also instructed: "If you must eat alone make sure you chew your food adequately, at least thirty chews per mouthful. Or else eat soft food that won't get caught in your throat. Eggs or soup are good choices. Pieces of bread should be no bigger than the nail on your little finger."

Terry agreed, adding that if food gets stuck in their throats while eating alone, they can save themselves by practising a self-inflicted form of the Heimlich manoeuvre. "You do this," he said, "by placing your fists on your chest and running into a wall."

I intervened. "I wouldn't advise running into a wall per se because a wall could damage your faces. Run into the *corner* of a wall instead, or into the edge of a table. And don't worry about breaking a rib. It will be worth it."

To drive the point home, I reminded them of the Christmas their father performed the Heimlich manoeuvre on the family dog, Mutz. She was choking on a chunk of stolen Christmas cake.

Mutz made it but was inconsolable for the next twelve years. She had understood: Death is a possibility.

67.

Puzzle of Acceptance

This puzzle tells us that our attempts to love the moment have not been going well because our lives are a jumble of woes nesting like rats in the attic, and the Rat Man was here but nothing came of it, and besides, we are sad about the gas bills we're having to pay because we've been running on vegetable oil for years.

This puzzle also tells us that we have never been cool and never won awards and are freighted by an undercurrent of dopiness but have been trained since birth to always tell the truth but tell it softly.

It further tells us that acceptance of this puzzle is what most therapists recommend. For us, though, the Puzzle of Acceptance does not surmount today's mood and its attendant world view, which is, namely, "What (and we can't stress this enough) the Fuck?"

68.

Today's Puzzle: Wet

Here is a picture of a wet road – large puddles, dividing line, cement curb – taken the same day our septic tank was pumped, and shortly after the pumping had finished. I was walking off a large feeling of shame. I took the picture to remind myself of an abiding puzzle: Why have we, once again, fallen below some random standard of decency?

The guy who did the pumping told us our septic tank was the worst-clogged septic tank he had ever seen.

It had been pumped only six years ago. How could that be?

"It was full of toilet paper," the pumper said with disgust. "Thick with it."

My face became hot. "I thought toilet paper deteriorated," I said.

"Apparently not," said Terry, and walked away, a stricken man.

The shame over the septic tank was the same shame I have felt at other times. The pet groomer, for example, who said our old cat Bob had the worst case of mats she'd ever seen, as if we'd been abusing him for years when we'd always loved Bob so much. And we *had* tried to stay on top of the mats; we had brushed him all the time. The groomer wasn't impressed.

It was the same with Sal, the man from Fidelity Carpet Cleaning, when he came to clean the one in the living room. He took one look at our old dog and said, "I smell urine." Out of shame we bought the more expensive "pet-proofing" package.

Shame is supposed to be one of the most devastating emotions, right up there with fear, hate, and revenge. But emotions, I am told, both the good and the bad ones, remain in our bodies for only ninety seconds before they dissolve like water vapour or smoke. Unless, of course, we feed them, especially the bad emotions, keeping them alive through obsessive thinking. Sometimes an old hurt or regret or rage remains for years as a time-devouring monster living within us, because we keep reliving the situation that caused the original monster to exist.

On the afternoon I took this picture I was clogged with shame. It's odd. I had always thought my life was going to be your run-of-the-mill fantasy musical about having babies. I hadn't counted on septic tanks, cat mats, or dog urine being part of the puzzle.

69.

With Reference to Cows 3

"Today," the cow says to me, "it feels good to be on this side of the fence."

"It feels good to be the cow that appears in your mind's eye while you sit at your desk ruminating over the hard questions."

"Unlike us, you will never know for certain what your existence means. You are obsessed with time and your attempts to slow it down. You are haunted and weep easily, are troubled and often make mistakes. You are always looking to  overpass your enlarging confusion. Cows like me understand your current frame of reference, one that is infused with news narratives, entertainment narratives, terror narratives."

"So it feels good to be on this side of the fence and anthropomorphizing about *you* for a change and showing care and interest in your well-being by offering solace, something everyone in the human family needs right now."

"Being a cow," the cow says, "you must be kind about it."

A puzzle about empathy.

70.

Whimsy Piece

The most popular jigsaw puzzles in the twenty-first century are not maps but images of dream landscapes, colourful birds, English country gardens, and every Disney cartoon character ever conceived.

According to Reader's Digest, *one of the world's hardest jigsaw puzzles is called "The Hunt." This puzzle of a thousand wooden pieces replicates an art nouveau painting by Robert Burns and contains a "tricky alternate solution," which is undisclosed. I can't imagine.*

The "world's hardest" puzzle is the Beverley micro jigsaw puzzle with the name of "Pure White Hell." It's advertised as having "tiny, same-sized pieces and a pure white image," which sounds to me like a description of poet Charles Simic's "memory-erasing room."

The largest commercially made puzzle in the world, according to the Ravensburger site, has 40,000 pieces and weighs forty-four pounds. Its title? "Memorable Disney Moments."

✚ *The fastest time for completing a thousand-piece puzzle in competition? Two hours, twenty-six minutes, and forty-five seconds. This must have been timed in a controlled setting supplied with water bottles and hand towels. Because of the frenzy.*

✚ *A jigsaw puzzle made by sixteen hundred students at the University of Economics Ho Chi Minh City in Vietnam consisted of 551,232 pieces and was completed by students on September 24, 2011. The puzzle depicted a lotus flower with six petals.*

71.

Puzzle of Space-Time Foam

There are many gods, the scientists now tell us. So many that there is one for each sentient being on the planet. The gods live in the space-time foam that is simultaneous with the space-time foam that we, singly, are living in. Your brother has his own space-time foam and god. Your mother. Your cat.

The space-time foam isn't frothy like dishwater bumbles, but clear, like the inside of a balloon. We and our gods exist within an infinite multi-bubble universe.

Sometimes our personal foam universe integrates with the foam universes belonging to our god, and when this happens, accidentally or in dreams, we find poetry, music, and the best parts of ourselves.

The hard part happens when we die – no surprise there – when our personal space-time foam disappears, poof, at the same instant we do. The god's foam, however, does not disappear, and neither does the god. Why not? It doesn't seem fair. But it's the same unfairness we've always endured – the gods have all the advantage.

This new theory tells us that after we die our gods hang around like huge mosquitoes looking for other lives to feed on.

"We are very inventive," the scientists say from their labs. "Making theories and following our minds. This is what we do."

They then went on to explain all the reasons for everything.

72.

With Reference to Cows 4

On sunny days they seem to wander like clouds above a meadow. At dusk, like mist around a thicket of trees.

When the weather is inclement, they float into the sky and rain down milk, cheering us up. We run outside with our buckets and pots then and give merry thanks.

To writer Annie Dillard, cows viewed on a hilltop looked to be "hung in catenary curves from their skeletons, like two-man tents." This is a true approximation. Cows camp out in themselves.

They are peaceful animals and seem to be followers of the Japanese philosopher Keiji Nishitani, who writes of having "intimate encounter[s] with everything that exists." Cows do this every moment of every day.

In the above drawing they are heading back to the barn after a day outside. At the approach, there is the feel of dirt between their hooves, the smell of disinfectant used for the milking machines, the annoyance of flies darting about their eyes.

There is the puzzle of myself as a peephole presence ...

73.

Puzzle of Aging

Early on I experienced the gigantic death-before-birth and began living the theme of what comes after.

Along the way I had my share of imaginary turns. I hacked up my mother with an adze. I was a serial arsonist. I got lost in a blizzard with a baby. I drank a cocktail made of aversion and glee – for years! – becoming like a robin trapped inside a chandelier, desperate to escape, desperate to stay.

After that I began staring at my face in the mirror. It was the mirror that told me there was nothing imaginary left. Flaring nostrils, disappearing eyebrows, panic lines overtaking laugh lines around my eyes and mouth.

I had never focused on the details of my face before. How has my face helped me get through life? How has it hindered?

You never know what people are going through and you never know how much they can benefit from a kind word.

A puzzle enigma.

74.

The Face

The face still wants to be beautiful, smiles warmly at itself in the bathroom mirror, deletes unflattering pictures it finds of itself on phones, turns its head away at the images, not wanting to look.

But sometimes it catches a glimpse of itself reflected in a shop window while it strides along as if it were thirty years ago, swinging its purse, long hair bouncing.

When this happens, it's a good day. The body clicks into alignment with its imagined version. The body feels strong. "You are beautiful," the body says to the face. The face beams!

Then it's "hello, hello," to one and all, radiating life.

The tall young cashier in the grocery store.

The handsome man in the library who thought she was the librarian.

The husband.

The cat.

75.

Today's Puzzle: Light

This is a picture of shadows through trees, many of which are leafless. They form a pattern on the road near our house. The lines and enclosed spaces and the sunlight, which is the sole reason the pattern occurs, present as another jigsaw puzzle on this cool winter's day. The roadside patches of mud and the cedar hedge, which are also streaked with light, play their part by giving the picture perspective.

"Everything is shown up by being expressed to the light, and whatever is expressed to the light itself becomes light," said Saint Paul in a quote used by Eckhart Tolle in *The Power of Now*.

This puzzle, in all its radiance, represents an instant of creation.

This puzzle stops me from fretting about the end of my world.

76.

The Grand Canyon

"It's pretty sweet, this place," said the twenty-five-year-old son on the camping trip. "Like the Manhattan of nature."

"The what?" said his father.

"The Manhattan of nature. Canyons that go on forever, changing in colour and rock type, the same way architecture changes in different neighbourhoods of New York."

Found puzzle, possibly about NDD, Nature Deficit Disorder.

77.

With Reference to Cows 5

The animal in the above drawing seems pleased to have its picture taken. It is a young steer, oblivious about what lies ahead. Isn't it handsome? And imagine the day – green pasture, spring sky!

We would love to call the steer "he," make of it something we could hug, but it is not a pet. It is without a personal pronoun, anonymous, one of a herd.

Most dairy cows are also part of a herd – a mega-dairy – but once they were singular, well-loved animals and given homey names like Mabel or Bessy. Today, they are anonymous milk producers; singing milkmaids and hay-filled stalls are a thing of the past. Instead, it is concrete floor enclosures, high-pressure water hoses, intimacy with a steel milking machine called the Rotolactor.

A dairy cow's productive lifespan is five years. After that they are turned into hamburger.

I recently read of a pig in Hong Kong that killed the butcher who was about to slaughter it. The tranquilizer had worn off and the pig attacked. A cleaver was involved. The butcher was about to wield it and, during the skirmish with the pig, the cleaver fell onto his leg, severing an artery.

What happened to the pig? Did it escape its fate like an action hero? The article didn't say. It left the story open-ended, but I think we can guess.

A puzzle about a dietary predicament that will not go away.

78.

Today's Puzzle: Shift

A bank of altocumulus clouds, sinking under its own weight, seems to touch the branches of a blossoming forsythia bush, which is made even more yellow by a brief flash of sunshine. It is midday and there is drama in this scene: the greyness of the clouds set against the sudden light, the curving road with cars parked in the distance leading you towards a darker, colder place.

These separate elements converge to present a confusion of effect, and yet the scene is a pleasing one. You have happened upon something beautiful.

If this were a jigsaw puzzle, there would be the balancing of the grey sky with the shadows on the road to contend with; the various greens, from the brightness of new grass alongside the ditch to the sombre green of mature evergreens; the thin strip of blue along the far hills.

The scene reminds me of how analytical a jigsaw puzzle is, the way it breaks apart the component elements of a scene or painting. And how difficult this is to do with emotions, especially the vibrant emotions, those of awe, for example, elicited by this scene of shifting light.

79.

Whimsy Piece: Puzzle Accessories

- *Puzzle boards with nonslip surfaces, raised edges, and four pull-out trays for storing sorted pieces*

- *Adhesive-backed puzzle mats that you can inflate to protect the work-in-progress and then roll up like a yoga mat*

- *Puzzle tables with tilting surfaces and a side board for sorting pieces*

- *Stackable sorting trays*

- *Puzzle glue containing adhesive and a lacquer so you can preserve your finished jigsaw and hang it on a wall*

- *Home Sweet Home Family Forever Puzzle Piece Interlocking Wall Plaque*

- *Puzzle stickers: adhesive-backed sheets that help in making a finished puzzle a frame*

- *Frames: "Decorate Every Moment!"*

- *Slippers, cardigan, eyeshade*

- *Eyeglass cleaner, magnifying glass*

- *Strong desk lamp, cats kept in another room*

- *Strong coffee/tea/Scotch*

- *Something to suck on*

- *Dr. Andrew Weil's 4-7-8 breathing technique*

80.

Jigsaw Danger

An online site, BrainsBreaker, sells software for PC and Mac computers that allows users to do away with tables and reading lamps and, instead, offers them the chance to "enjoy the experience of doing jigsaw puzzles comfortably and safely" on their computers.

The program lets you make a personalized jigsaw puzzle of any image you want – your dog, your wedding, your Christmas turkey. You can create a puzzle of only four pieces or a thousand pieces, move them around using a mouse, and save your effort so you can open it another day.

It makes sense. Who takes a partially finished jigsaw puzzle on a bus, a plane, in the car to get gas? Who sits with a jigsaw puzzle on a tray on their lap while attending a municipal council meeting? Exactly – no one. This is why BrainsBreaker is offering a computer version. It is neat, portable, and the jigsaw can be assembled anywhere.

But the notion of doing a computer jigsaw "safely and comfortably" raises for me the question of safety for regular jigsaw puzzlers. Are there places of assembly that are uncomfortable and dangerous? If you're not working on a jigsaw in your home, which if you are lucky is free of discomfort and danger, where are these threatening *other* places?

An institution comes to mind. One, say, in which a puzzle called "Simpler Times" has been set up in the activity room of a long-term care home for the residents' pleasure. The puzzle's image shows a farm family in 1937 having a picnic on a balmy summer's day, mounds of hay in the background and ripe yellow plums on a nearby tree.

But perhaps an institutional activity room is an unsafe place to put a jigsaw puzzle. Perhaps the puzzler is in danger of assault and degradation there. Maybe some of the residents will become hotly jealous of sanctimonious Mr. M., who is hogging the puzzle time and leaving no room for anyone else to enjoy it, the puzzle becoming a focal point for social discord.

Puzzle danger could abound in such a place. There might be a mad person on the loose, resident, staff, or visitor, who sabotages puzzle completion by hiding pieces throughout the building – in flower pots, under chair cushions, in pill cups. So that along with a resident's nightly pharmaceuticals, a person gets a specimen-coloured centrepiece. Or a piece of blue sky appears with a serving of the "Chef's Choice" entrée – yesterday's stew on toast – in the dining room at dinner. An angry comment about the food?

The final indignity to the puzzle would be its disappearance by management to the safety of the damp basement because, by then, the puzzle, no matter how homey and simple, would have become annoying to have around.

Writing about computer-generated jigsaw puzzles makes me nostalgic for the living-room setup. You pause by the puzzle on your way to unload the dishwasher, hover for a couple of minutes, place the piece that has taken you days to find, feel a pop of satisfaction, carry on.

81.

History

A morning disappears while I'm fitting together a jigsaw by the Waterford Puzzle Company from their Old Masters series called "The Siesta," the painting by Gauguin.

Judging by the range of pleasurable emotions I've been having while piecing together the women in this puzzle, as well as the feelings of frustration and doubt that intrude, I could be writing this book.

Another morning disappears while working on a jigsaw called "Queen Mary's Dolls' House, Windsor Castle." The puzzle measures four by six inches and is miniature in size to match its subject. It has eighty pieces, regular-sized, and since it's a Wentworth puzzle, there are several whimsy pieces included: a crown, a lion, a violin, a vase, a sword. It was given to me by Mary, the wife of Terry's friend Morley. She found it in a local thrift store.

The puzzle was created in 2000 as part of the Wentworth Royal Collection and is copyrighted by Her Majesty Queen Elizabeth II. The information on the back of the box states that the wooden pieces are cut from Finnish birch ply "in patterns that challenge, intrigue, frustrate, and confuse." The puzzle image of the dollhouse shows an "upstairs-downstairs" format – a formal parlour above, a servant's kitchen below. The lowest level of the puzzle is the entrance way to the house – four cypress trees bank a large, ornate gate. It's a commemorative piece meant to mark an era and to last generations, even though "commemoration" is no longer something many people consider an appropriate response to the UK's colonial past.

82.

Puzzle of Nothing

Two painters had become bored with their subjects – daffodils, dogs, marinas.

Then, by chance, they read a quote by artist Mary Pratt that appeared in her obituary: "My only strength is finding something where most people would find nothing."

Because of the effect this quote had on them, they decided to spend the rest of their lives looking closely at nothing, believing they had found the doorway to the sublime.

So far there is nothing of interest in this puzzle. Mainly it is Rolf working doggedly on a painting of his bathtub, Rita sketching in trash at the top of the driveway, some beige shading in the background.

But then the puzzle begins to shimmer. This is because Rita looks up and sees *something* where before she had always seen nothing of interest – the sky. She sees a towering cumulus cloud backlit by the sun. The cloud *sears her sensations.*

"The real secret of the arts," said Zen master Shunryū Suzuki (鈴木 俊隆), is to "always be a beginner."

When you finish this puzzle there will be nothing there.

83.

Whimsy Piece

My friend Milly spent the winter working on the mighty one-thousand-piece puzzle called "The World of Shakespeare." It comes with a poster identifying the important theatrical figures in the image. Milly took puzzle satisfaction to a higher level when she said, "It's the endorphin hit that happens when you place a random piece you weren't looking for. It's called the puzzler's high. It gives you an energizing, glow-y outlook on life."

84.

Today's Puzzle: Submerged

Once again, cracks in the road suggest a jigsaw puzzle. This one is partly submerged by a puddle. It rained last night after a spell of cold, dry weather but the daily temperature is beginning to rise. It's the last day of February in a year that's not leaping anywhere. Crocuses are in bloom in neighbourhood gardens and daffodils are in bud.

This morning I hung towels outside to dry. Because of the sudden warmth, I wore a sweater to do this and not a coat and hat. The thrill I experienced was outstanding.

This partially submerged puzzle reminds me of what is often hidden from understanding.

Dreams, for example. I suppose it's because I've been looking at road surfaces a lot, but last night I had a dream in which I was appointed Writer Laureate of the road we live on. It's a short road of two blocks lined with maybe twenty houses. Who appointed me Writer Laureate? I don't know. It's a mystery. But there is nothing anyone can do about a mystery except surrender to it.

Sometimes life is incredible!

85.

Puzzle of Clairvoyance

In the 1948 Italian film *Bicycle Thieves*, director Vittorio De Sica considers the puzzle of clairvoyance.

The film follows the plight of Antonio Ricci, a poor labourer, who, desperate for help, waits with a long line of seekers on a clairvoyant's tenement stairs. He is there to visit the bedridden La Santona.

When it's his turn, Antonio Ricci creeps into the room. La Santona is propped up with pillows. Her daughter takes his money.

"What have they stolen?" La Santona asks.

"My bike," Antonio Ricci says.

La Santona says, "What can I say? I can only tell you what I see. Listen: you'll find it straight away or not at all. Understand? You'll find it straight away or not at all. Keep your eyes open.

Antonio Ricci says, "Where, straight away?"

La Santona says, "How should I know? Go and try to understand what I said. You'll find it straight away or not at all."

The clairvoyant was right, as they sometimes are. Antonio Ricci did not find his bicycle straight away. And then he never found his bicycle.

This is a fragile, neorealism puzzle.

Proceed as if wrapped in gauze.

86.

Puzzle of Nowhere to Go

It was a long climb to reach the top of the mountain, two dirty children leading the way. I was carrying a garbage bag filled with our belongings. We were haggard, careworn, afraid. Below, the town lay in ruins. We found an empty shed in which to shelter.

Then the director yelled "cut" and told us to go home because it was getting dark. The children went off with their parents.

At home a baby shower was in progress. It was packed with guests drinking Prosecco. I overheard a young woman, the future aunt, say, "I'm so excited about being an aunt. It's my first shot and I think I'll be good at it. Having kids of my own, not so much."

She got so drunk she had to be carried off to an upstairs bedroom.

Shortly after, we heard a terrific boom and saw a blinding flash of white light in the sky to the west.

"A nuclear bomb!" I screamed, and everyone else at the shower screamed, too. But the director, who was still hanging about, didn't react. He was sitting on the couch beside the retro lamp calmly smoking a cigarette.

I wanted him to say "cut!" but he didn't. Instead he said, "Nowhere to go."

I was scared for Monty, my albino squirrel, who was chattering, banging himself against his cage. So I grabbed the cage and ran with it into the night, away from the flash. For Monty's sake I had to make a run for it. I had to save him, didn't I?

A puzzling nightmare.

87.

Puzzle of Endings

"In life, the number of beginnings is exactly equal to the number of endings: no one has yet to begin a life who will not end it," writes Mary Ruefle. This quote comes from an essay of hers called "On Beginnings." Who can argue with this statement?

Our neighbours Rory and Eileen, now in their seventies, told us their terminating gesture will be to take their two Gordon setters with them after consuming a bottle of Scotch malt and then driving their car very fast into the first concrete wall they can find. It was a lovely afternoon in May when they casually revealed their plan to us over their garden fence. Early roses were in bloom, and yellow tulips. Initially, our chat had been about getting rid of dead things in the garden.

"We'll all go out together," said Rory happily, referring to their chosen end. They don't have children.

"Yes, but well, maybe not too soon," Eileen said.

Having the end in sight has seldom been part of anyone's personal narrative, though we've always had a suspicion that one day the end would come. This suspicion returns in later years with a force and is as fresh as the deepest insight. Even so, most of us are hoping to hold off the inevitable; we haven't come to the end of our storytelling cycle yet.

Queen Elizabeth II, visiting the set of *Coronation Street* in 2021, said to the assembled cast and crew, though she could have been giving a confirming statement to those of us assembled at the abyss, "It's really marvellous you've been able to carry on."

88.

Today's Puzzle: Rocks

A combination of broken concrete slabs, rocks, and large driftwood makes up this jumble, which appeared along a beach path on a cool, spring day. The tide was high, leaving only a narrow strip of sand and pebbles to walk on.

As a jigsaw puzzle, it would be difficult to assemble. The beige and grey colours of the materials would meld together with the eroding bank, the scrub, distant evergreens, and blue sky offering the only contrast to the subtleness of the colours. There is a haphazard feel to the scene.

I am making a mental puzzle of these rocks and driftwood because of something Bashō wrote over three hundred years ago that I have long questioned. He mentions in his travelogue "A Visit to Sarashina Village" that he became "filled with desire" to see the full moon over Mount Obasute at the rugged mountain village of Sarashina. This is where, he also noted, villagers in the remote past abandoned their aged mothers among the rocks.

I am unable to get past the abandoned aged mothers every time I read the account, and I am stalled there again today. Did the mothers go to the rocks willingly? Did they experience their destination with resignation or calm? The word "abandoned" suggests otherwise.

The average Japanese lifespan in 1689 was forty-three years. Bashō, at the time he wrote his travelogue, would have been close to this age and considered an old man. An aged woman at the time of her abandonment in the "remote past" may have been the same age or slightly older, perhaps in her late forties.

I am revisiting the puzzle of the abandoned mothers on the rocks today because it is my birthday and I'm miles past the age of forty-three.

I am not expecting to become an abandoned mother anytime soon.

Though you never know.

I have begun to see the hard, haphazard rocks in the distance.

89.

Notes on the Jigsaw Book

Again, you could say that each person's life is like a jigsaw puzzle and that the pieces are continually changing. You could further say that this is what it feels like to be alive right now, that you are living inside your personal puzzle; each piece is a puzzle unto itself; sometimes it fits into a coherent whole, and sometimes it does not.

"Life flies at us in bright splinters," wrote Lance Olsen in his novel *10:01*.

Yes, and it is impossible to remember all the pieces. They become forgotten memories wheeling beyond the edges of our lives.

"Memory is continually created, a story told and retold, using jigsaw pieces of experience," said Jenny Diski in her memoir *Skating to Antarctica*.

"Memory is a lunatic props-mistress," said Annie Ernaux in *her* memoir *A Girl's Story*.

You can hope, as Tony Hoagland expressed in his poem "Questions of Influence," that a book or poem might come along

> to calm everybody down
> explaining how the pieces fit perfectly together:
> how everything
> moves through the crowd of everything else
> touching and whispering and changing.

How are the pieces of our lives – the fragments – weighted, we ask? Does trauma define our lives, does wonder, thankfulness? Are confusion, sorrow, love, loss, and happiness represented in equal measure, or do just a few pieces dominate – the highlights and lowlights, the births, graduations, weddings, illnesses, deaths? And what of the in-betweens? The blurred and forgotten pieces of life that remain unconnected? The "bright vignettes in a waste of forgotten time" is what John Gray called them in *Straw Dogs: Thoughts on Humans and Other Animals*. What of these? The waiting in lineups and traffic, shopping for groceries, watering plants, feeding animals, staring out windows. The daily sweeping and tidying up; the washing of clothes, floors, dishes, children; the preparation of food; the times we are sick. The worrying over money or sex that goes on day after day throughout the years. Do they end up in the vacuum cleaner we use to tidy up our lives? And what of the holes this leaves in the puzzle?

If things go well during our brilliant and confusing lives, there is a textured blend of young and old, heart and edge. It's today and tomorrow, and try not to be a jerk. At best, it can be what Dan Wakefield, a friend of Kurt Vonnegut, once said about him; it's worth repeating: "He laughed a lot and was kind to everyone."

I thought I would ask my friend and neighbour Phil for his thoughts on the third year of the pandemic. At the start of it, in 2020, when we were in lockdown, he had said from the end of his driveway, "Man, this is like living through the slowest sci-fi movie ever."

Three years later I sent him an email. I wanted to know if he still felt the same way about where we were regarding the pandemic, or had he moved on to another mindset? "And yes," I said, "I'm fishing," and told him about this book I was writing.

"A jigsaw puzzle, yeah," he said a few days later in reply. "That's turning out to be one of the essential metaphors for our addled COVID–climate changing times. We have the big picture from the box cover, but no idea how anything connects. We have the necessary pieces to put it all together (box now open) but no plan (cover's been misplaced) as to how to make it all connect. The next part is a little more nuanced. There are pieces missing. They show up one day but not the next. They can't get across that jigsaw border. We kind of didn't see all these waves coming and can only wonder (so far) what will show up next ..."

For the past three years we have only seen Phil and his wife Melinda on walks or from the end of their driveway, even though they live seven houses away. Or we see pictures on Facebook of Melinda's latest painting, of their grandchildren, of Phil's reno to the front of their house. For years we partied with them and other neighbour friends every couple of months. Played the music loud, danced all over the houses, drank and smoked too much.

Walking through the smoke from the wildfires this past summer, it occurred to me that we needn't blame the jigsaw puzzle for being what it is, which is something reassuringly finite and controllable against all odds, unlike the political upheavals worldwide and the extreme weather events we've been experiencing on the northwest coast of North America – heat domes, atmospheric rivers, extreme freezing temperatures, and more snow than we're used to.

90.

Three Questions

First: *What happens to a finished puzzle?*

We think we know the answer: it's returned to its box or, in rare cases, it's varnished and hung on a wall. But if it's not to be hung, how long is it allowed to remain "finished," to be on display? What is the average amount of time? A couple of days, weeks?

Second: *Is there something unseemly going on when the jigsaw is finally pulled apart?*

Could it be seen as an act of destruction? Are you ruining something you thought you had created? Has an embarrassing secret been exposed? That you are not the artist you imagined yourself to be, that you're merely the assembler, even though hours spent working on a jigsaw puzzle can pass like the rapture you felt while doing a paint-by-number kit – like I did as a child, a picture of the heroic dog Rin Tin Tin, carefully painting in the proud browns and blacks of his face?

Third: *Should puzzles be recycled?*

In our neighbourhood on recycling day, a woman driving a white Toyota stops at all the blue boxes before the truck arrives. She takes the wine, vodka, and gin bottles, pop and beer cans. I had always wondered what she was up to when I passed by her on my walks. Her open trunk is neatly organized into six sorting areas. "I'm collecting for schools in Lesotho," she told me when I finally asked. "Last year we made twelve thousand dollars. There are three of us collecting. We help pay for uniforms, books, and teachers."

Derek is another neighbour who frequents the blue boxes. He rides an ancient three-speed everywhere. He inherited waterfront property from his father and is rumoured to be brilliant because he has three Ph.D.s – in Physics, Environmental Studies, and something else. Because he is dishevelled and has worn the same beige jacket for years, he presents as a man who is barely scraping by.

Derek takes the beer and pop cans if he can get to them before the Lesotho woman. He rides his bike defiantly without a helmet. He never speaks to you or acknowledges your existence as he rides by after stuffing his pack. I'm guessing he's on his way to the bottle depot to cash in the cans for money to buy food.

"Don't be so sure," Terry says. "He could be one of those loners with millions in the bank."

By midmorning on recycling day, all the glass and pop and beer cans will be gone. I always glance at the blue boxes containing paper, which remain full. No one takes the paper. And no one recycles jigsaw puzzles with their sockets, knobs, and locks against everyday distress.

91.

Today's Puzzle: Delicate

Mud again. This time it occurs as small puddles in the middle of a delicate road puzzle, an exquisite configuration of lines, shading, and rainwater. As a jigsaw it is temporary and will never be solved. There is nothing about it to understand. It is perfect.

This puzzle teaches me about beauty.

"The truly precious things are those forming ladders reaching towards the beauty of the world," wrote Elaine Scarry in *On Beauty and Being Just*. Scarry was quoting from Simone Weil's book, *Waiting for God*.

"No mud, no lotus," wrote Zen master Thích Nhất Hạnh.

Thinking of mud, I sent the following quote to my friend Jane. It's by Zen master Rinzai from the twelfth century. For me, it sums up the experience of being present to myself in the world, something I am trying to do more and more of these days:

What, at this moment, is lacking?

Jane's answer: "What's missing is ecstasy."

I laughed. But I'm still thinking about her answer. I always pay close attention to what Jane says because the connections hidden in many of her comments are often profound. I think in this instance, though, she was being ironic with her answer because her life had many demands on it just then, and ecstasy would have been a welcome alternative.

The answer to the quote, if I understand it correctly, is that the moment is lacking nothing. It is complete unto itself. Ecstasy, when it occurs or doesn't occur, has as much weight as anything else that may arise.

A similar question in the Zen tradition:

If not now, when?

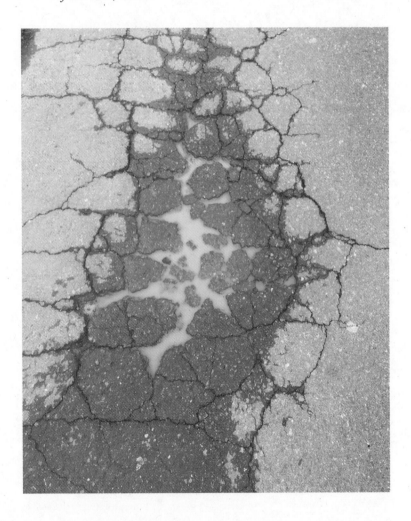

92.

Today's Puzzle: Tire Tracks

This puzzle of muddy tire tracks at the side of a road has something to do with my being twenty-four-years old and driving with my boyfriend in his pickup truck along the West Coast Road into Victoria. "The impulse to remember" is the phrase this puzzle recalls.

It was dusk and raining hard and we were delivering wood to a guy who had answered the ad in the newspaper. *Full cord of alder. $35. Delivery included.*

The wood was from my boyfriend's property – he wasn't hard up – and he'd cheated. It wasn't a full cord as advertised, but half a cord, a pickup load.

The customer, an older man, came outside with a measuring stick after we had dumped the wood, discovered the lie, and refused the delivery. "That's not a full cord," he said. "And it's green wood. Useless."

How can I move in the direction of what I sense – not as a butterfly, but as a poet?

This years-later quote by American poet Kay Ryan distills for me what was going on at the time, something I could not articulate then. My life was a puzzle, not fully understood, but it had something to do with judging a person's character and finding it wanting, and something to do with being impelled towards the ineffable, the golden, the shimmering.

93.

Endpiece

End of the road for the yellow line.

Postscript

The clouds were below with the puzzle of the past.
Bits of the world clicked into place.

—FANNY HOWE
Love and I (2019)

Sources and Notes

1. *Whimsy Piece*
   "Why the Jigsaw Puzzle Industry Deserves a Place in the Sun," Jigsaw Puzzle International Convention blog, October 31, 2021, jpic.club /why-the-jigsaw-puzzle-industry-deserves-its-place-in-the-sun/.

2. **Puzzle States**
   Angelica Pajovic, "The Puzzling Mind: How Doing Jigsaw Puzzles Can Help Us Focus on Each Moment," The Mindful Word, April 19, 2017, www.themindfulword.org/2017/puzzling-mind-jigsaw -puzzles/.

   Georges Perec, *Life A User's Manual*, trans. David Belos (Boston: David R. Godine, 1987).

   Harry Mathews and Alastair Brotchie, eds., *Oulipo Compendium* (London: Atlas Press, 1998).

   Note: The Twitter limit of using no more than 280 characters per tweet, including glyphs, URLs, hashtags, and emojis, is an unintentional form of Oulipo restraint.

3. **Regular Puzzle Pieces**
   Perec, *Life A User's Manual*.

4. **Puzzle for Brains**
   Note: Agatha Christie was writing during the height of the jigsaw craze in the first half of the twentieth century and not one of her sixty-six detective novels feature a death-by-jigsaw puzzle. This is particularly odd because her signature technique is the detective's

culminating revelation to the assembled suspects of the pieces of the puzzle everyone else has missed.

9. **Infinity Puzzle**
Mary Ruefle, "On Beginnings," *Madness, Rack, and Honey: Collected Lectures* (Seattle: Wave Books, 2012).

Note: Mary Ruefle is her own beautiful bird, flies her own way. In one of her book's essays, "Twenty-Two Short Lectures," she has this free-standing entry:

Short Lecture Enacting the Inner Life of a Poet

(Play electronic man screaming, "McKenna's lost his dog, Captain!" alternating with birdsong whistle)

Harry Dean Stanton, "It's all a movie anyway," Juvenile Cinephile on Tumblr, July 14, 2015, juvenilecinephile.tumblr.com/post /124119701319/you-get-older-in-the-end-you-end-up-accepting.

10. **A Piece of Sue's Puzzle**
Photo by Susan Kerr.

11. **Notes on the Biscuit Puzzle**
Frank Zappa, "The crux of the biscuit," is from his album *The Crux of the Biscuit* (Zappa Records, 2016).

Casa Omnia, casaomnia.it/en/.

Ciara Knight, "26 British Biscuits Ranked from Worst to Best," Joe (website), August 14, 2018, www.joe.co.uk/food/26-british-biscuits -ranked-worst-best-194778.

"On average, the British population eats eleven biscuits a week": Nils-Gerrit Wunsch, "Average Purchase per Person per Week of Biscuits and Crispbread in the United Kingdom (UK) from 2006 to 2020/2021, by Type (in Grams)," Statista, April 11, 2023, www.statista.com/statistics/380355/weekly-uk-household -consumption-of-biscuits-united-kingdom-by-type/.

Stephen Hall, *The Raw Shark Texts* (New York: HarperCollins, 2007).

Neil Gaiman, *American Gods* (New York: William Morrow, 2001).

12. **Not a Puzzle**
Photo by Terry Farrant.

13. *Whimsy Piece*
John Spilsbury's map, "Europe Divided into Its Kingdoms, Etc.," is in the public domain and can be found at en.wikipedia.org/wiki/John _Spilsbury_(cartographer).

16. **Tiny Heaven**
Maira Kalman, *The Principles of Uncertainty* (New York: Penguin Books, 2007).

18. **Puzzle of Art**
Louise Bourgeois is mentioned in Kalman's book.

Note: A book that Maira Kalman playfully illustrates is the fifth edition of William Strunk Jr. and E.B. White's guide to writing, *The Elements of Style*, which focuses on the principles of composition and the use of correct grammar.

I don't remember being charmed by the wit found in this book when I first read it at university, but I have since found many examples. Here is one: in the section "Words and Expressions Commonly Misused" the advice is: "Do not ... say 'I feel nauseous,' unless you are sure you have that effect on people."

The highlight in this latest edition, though, is Kalman's illustrations. A killing example appears in the section "Enclose Parenthetic Expressions between Commas."

Against a sweetly pink background is a full-page portrait of a basset hound. The dog looks exasperated. The caption beneath the portrait – an example of correct comma usage – reads,

Well, Susan, this is a fine mess you are in.

William Strunk Jr. and E.B. White, *The Elements of Style Illustrated*, illus. Maria Kalman (New York: Penguin Books, 2007).

19. *Whimsy Piece*
    Ellis Rosin, "How to Stay Optimistic" (cartoon) *New Yorker*,
    February 7, 2022, www.newyorker.com/magazine/2022/02/07
    /how-to-stay-optimistic.

21. **Notes on the Great Puzzle**
    Charles Simic, *Dime-Store Alchemy: The Art of Joseph Cornell* (New
    York: NYRB Classics, 2011).

    Note: I am beginning to understand the allure, the need, the desire,
    the *necessity* of jigsaw puzzles. Not a theory or a system, a jigsaw
    puzzle can be experienced as a material thing nestled in the universe,
    and tiny, like us. This feels companionable.

    Note: "Herb is for the healing of the nation; herb is for the
    meditation; herb is for the higher vibrations," said Bob Marley's son
    Rohan about the family's new cannabis paraphernalia business. "We
    [see] it as a spiritual thing, given to us by God," said Marley's widow,
    Rita. Daniel Kreps, "Official Bob Marley Marijuana Blend on the
    Way," *Rolling Stone*, November 19, 2014, www.rollingstone.com
    /music/music-news/official-bob-marley-marijuana-blend-on-the
    -way-204612/.

23. **Puzzle of Chainsaw Yoga**
    With a sly nod to Gail Bradshaw, esteemed yoga teacher.

24. *Whimsy Piece*
    Cambridge Advanced Learner's Dictionary & Thesaurus, Cambridge
    University Press, s.v. "nerd," accessed May 2023, dictionary.cambridge
    .org/dictionary/english/nerd.

25. **The Merry View**
    Caroline Sykes, "Celebrity Beasts," www.carolinesykes.co.uk/celebs
    /celebs.html.

    Hannah Frishberg, "Son's Brutal Obit of His 'Plus-Sized, Redneck'
    Mother Goes Viral," *New York Post*, December 16, 2021, nypost.com
    /2021/12/16/sons-brutal-obit-of-his-plus-sized-redneck-mom-goes
    -viral/.

The other obituaries appeared in the *Victoria Times Colonist.*

27. **Puzzle of Finland**
The wedding toast is from Wikipedia's entry "Toast (honor),"
en.wikipedia.org/wiki/Toast_(honor).

28. **Song**
Josh Jones, "George Harrison Explains Why Everyone Should Play
the Ukulele," Open Culture, August 5, 2014, www.openculture.com
/2014/08/george-harrison-explains-why-everyone-should-play-the
-ukulele-with-words-and-music.html.

29. **F. Scott Fitzgerald's Song**
Edmund Wilson, *The Twenties: From Notebooks and Diaries of the
Period* (New York: Farrar, Straus and Giroux, 2019).

30. **Veiled Meanings**
Tony Hoagland, "The Third Dimension," *Priest Turned Therapist
Treats Fear of God* (Minneapolis: Greywolf Press, 2018).

32. **Today's Puzzle: Yellow Line**
Margaret Drabble, *The Pattern in the Carpet: A Personal History with
Jigsaws* (New York: Houghton Mifflin Harcourt, 2009).

35. **Puzzle of Dogs**
A version of the dog-and-flea quote can be found in Virginia Woolf,
Flush: A Biography (London: Penguin Little Black Classics, 2017).

37. **Puzzle of Alice Who Is over One Hundred and Fifty-Eight Years Old**
Lewis Carroll, *Alice's Adventures in Wonderland and Through the
Looking-Glass* (New York: Chartwell Books, 2021).

39. **Today's Puzzle: Scales**
The Leonard Cohen quote is from "Thanks for the Dance," track 4 on
Thanks for the Dance (Columbia Legacy, 2019).

Matsuo Bashō 松尾 芭蕉, *Backroads to Far Towns: Bashō's Travel
Journal,* trans. Cid Corman and Kamaike Susumu (Buffalo: White
Pine Press, 2004).

40. **A Day at the Beach**
Mary Oliver, "Of Power and Time," *Upstream: Selected Essays* (New York: Penguin Books, 2019).

Note: "A brick on your wrist is not what a fashionable person is going to wear this fall." This is something a fashion magazine once hurled at me. I was at the height of my overfocusing on time and found it greatly affirming.

42. **Notes on the Desiccated Old Masters**
Online site selling Old Masters jigsaw puzzles: steamcommunity .com/app/1368750.

Aldous Huxley, *The Doors of Perception and Heaven and Hell* (New York: Harper Perennial Modern Classics, 2009).

Note: About the Shiki haiku, found in *The Doors of Perception*, Huxley wrote, "Shiki's *haiku* (which I quote in R.H. Blyth's translation) expresses, by indirection, exactly what I then felt – the excessive, the too obvious glory of the flowers, as contrasted with the subtler miracle of their foliage."

43. **Other Puzzles**
Virginia Graham, *Say Please* (London: Harvill Press, 1954).

Note: In the foreword to her book, Graham wrote: "This is a book on etiquette for ladies, neither of which or whom now exists ... But it may make you laugh, which is always nice. It may, of course, do nothing of the kind, which will be an enormous pity."

44. **Cube**
Mike DiCenzo, "Fran Lebowitz's One Star Amazon Reviews," *New Yorker*, January 22, 2021, www.newyorker.com/humor/daily-shouts /fran-lebowitzs-one-star-amazon-reviews.

46. **Cross Words**
Jordan Reid and Erin Williams, *The Big Activity Book for Anxious People* (New York: Penguin Books, 2019).

Note: What Maggie Nelson *actually* said in her much-admired book is: "I am interested in having three orifices stuffed full of thick, veiny cock." Maggie Nelson, *Bluets* (Seattle: Wave Books, 2009).

47. **Today's Puzzle: Path**
Bashō, *Backroads to Far Towns.*

48. **Notes on Roads**
Ken McLeod, *Reflections on Silver River: Tokmé Zongpo's "Thirty-Seven Practices of a Bodhisattva"* (Los Angeles: Unfettered Mind Media, 2014).

Kurt Lewin and Jean-Paul Sartre on hodological space: "Hodological Space," Wikipedia, en.wikipedia.org/wiki/Hodological_space.

Dōgen's "Death Poem" is frequently quoted and can easily be found online at, for example, thedewdrop.org/2020/09/02/dogen -death-poem/.

Golden Mean image by Spencer Williams.

"A true Zen saying" is from Frank Zappa and the Mothers, "Dummy Up," track 3 on *Roxy & Elsewhere* (DiscReet Records, 1974).

51. **Puzzle of Faith**
David Shields, *Reality Hunger: A Manifesto* (New York: Knopf, 2010).

56. *Whimsy Piece*
"Lead to clearer and more precise thinking" is from Adrienne Santos-Longhurst, "Everything You Need to Know about Sensory Deprivation Tank Therapy," Healthline, updated April 24,2023, www.healthline.com/health/sensory-deprivation-tank.

57. **Puzzle of Youth**
"The 'cherry pie is a miracle'" is taken from the TV series *Twin Peaks.* It was spoken by the Log Lady, actor Catherine E. Coulson. *Twin Peaks*, 1990–1991 and 2017, was created by Mark Frost and David Lynch.

62. Notes on Boredom

David Foster Wallace, *The Pale King* (New York: Little, Brown and Company, 2011).

Jean Baudrillard, *Cool Memories IV*, trans. Chris Turner (New York: Verso, 2003).

Joseph Brodsky, "Listening to Boredom," *Harper's Magazine* 290, no. 1738 (March 1, 1995), www.thefreelibrary.com/Listening+to +boredom.-a016514287.

Meghan Holohan, "There Are 5 Types of Boredom, According to Researchers," Mental Floss, December 2013, www.mentalfloss.com /article/54074/there-are-5-types-boredom.

Note: Inside the box five hundred jigsaw puzzle pieces are lumped together in a clear plastic bag. Mostly, what shows through the plastic are the undersides of the pieces, which are dull grey, like broken bits of boredom.

The plastic bag is sealed, as if to indicate that pilfering has not taken place; that there will be no missing pieces; that all will be well with the assembly; that we can trust the outcome, in this case, the reconstructed picture on the cover of the box: Dirt Road.

Once again, I am joining 9.4 million people worldwide who, in any given moment, are working on a jigsaw puzzle. This remains an unsettling thought.

65. Darkness

Antoine de Saint-Exupéry, *The Little Prince*, trans. Katherine Woods (New York: Mariner Books, 2000).

66. Jigsaw Death

Note: How to perform the Heimlich manoeuvre
Stand behind a choking person and slightly to one side. Support their chest with one hand.
Give up to five sharp blows between their shoulder blades with the heel of your hand.
Check if the blockage has cleared.

If not, give up to five abdominal thrusts.

Because of the increasingly controversial nature of Dr. Heimlich's personality and the validity of some of his research, the American Red Cross and the American Heart Association decided, in 1995, to rename the Heimlich manoeuvre the "abdominal thrust."

Question: What did Dr. Henry Heimlich do to warrant the erasure of his name?

Answer: By some accounts, he hogged the acclaim surrounding the manoeuvre by not acknowledging his colleague, Edward Patrick, as co-creator; made fraudulent (unsubstantiated) claims about the manoeuvre's success rate ("I have saved fifty thousand lives!"); and seems to have been a defective father. Said his second son, Peter Heimlich: He was "a spectacular con man and a serial liar" ("Henry Heimlich," Wikipedia, en.wikipedia.org /wiki/Henry_Heimlich).

Problematic as a human being, then. Not a well-liked person.

"There is weakness inherent in the word *not*," Strunk and White suggest in *The Elements of Style*.

A "not" person, then.

69. **With Reference to Cows 3**
Photo by Terry Farrant.

70. *Whimsy Piece*
Guinness World Records, "Fastest Time to Complete a 1,000-Piece Jigsaw Puzzle in Competition," guinnessworldrecords.com /world-records/688903-fastest-time-to-complete-a-1-000-piece -jigsaw-puzzle-in-competition.

"Memory-erasing room" is from Simic, *Dime-Store Alchemy*.

Guinness World Record News, "Vietnam Puts Together the World's Largest Jigsaw Puzzle," October 10, 2011, www .guinnessworldrecords.com/news/2011/10/vietnam-puts-together -the-world%E2%80%99s-largest-jigsaw-puzzle/.

72. **With Reference to Cows 4**
The Keiji Nishitani quote is from Kyle Chayka, "Being in Nothingness," *Harper's Magazine* December 2019, harpers.org /archive/2019/12/the-longing-for-less-living-with-minimalism-kyle -chayka/.

Annie Dillard, *The Writing Life* (New York: Harper & Row, 1989).

75. **Today's Puzzle: Light**
Eckhart Tolle, *The Power of Now: A Guide to Spiritual Enlightenment* (Vancouver: Namaste Publishing, 1997).

76. **The Grand Canyon**
Timothy Egan with Casey Egan, "Can the Selfie Generation Unplug and Get into Parks?" *National Geographic*, October 2016, www.nationalgeographic.com/magazine/article/unplugging-the -selfie-generation-national-parks.

82. **Puzzle of Nothing**
Canadian Press, "Mary Pratt, Acclaimed East Coast Painter, Dead at 83," August 15, 2018, beyondthedash.com/obituary/mary -pratt-1067531803.

Shunryū Suzuki 鈴木 俊隆, *Zen Mind, Beginner's Mind: Informal Talks on Zen Meditation and Practice* (Boulder: Shambhala, 1970).

85. **Puzzle of Clairvoyance**
Bicycle Thieves, dir. Vittorio De Sica (Rome: Produzioni De Sica, 1948).

87. **Puzzle of Endings**
Ruefle, "On Beginnings," *Madness, Rack, and Honey.*

"It's really marvellous" is from BBC News, "Queen Visits Coronation Street Set to Mark 60 Years of Soap," July 8, 2021, www.bbc.com/news/uk-england-manchester-57764192.

88. **Today's Puzzle: Rocks**
"Visit to Sarashina Village" appears in Matsuo Bashō, *The Narrow*

Road to the Deep North and Other Travel Sketches, trans. Nobuyuki Yuasa (New York: Penguin Books, 1967).

89. **Notes on the Jigsaw Book**
Lance Olsen, *10:01* (Portland: Chiasmus, 2005).

Jenny Diski, *Skating to Antarctica: A Journey to the End of the World* (London: Virago, 2005).

Annie Ernaux, *A Girl's Story*, trans. Alison Strayer (New York: Seven Stories Press, 2020).

Tony Hoagland, "Questions of Influence," *Recent Changes in the Vernacular* (New Mexico: Tres Chicas Books, 2017).

John Gray, *Straw Dogs: Thoughts on Humans and Other Animals* (London: Granta, 2002).

91. **Today's Puzzle: Delicate**
Elaine Scarry, *On Beauty and Being Just* (Princeton, NJ: Princeton University Press, 1999).

Thích Nhất Hạnh, *No Mud, No Lotus: The Art of Transforming Suffering* (Berkeley: Parallax Press, 2014).

"What, at this moment, is lacking?" is quoted in Tolle, *The Power of Now*, p. 43.

"If not now, when?" attributed to Hillel the Elder in McLeod, *Reflections on Silver River*.

92. **Today's Puzzle: Tire Tracks**
Kay Ryan, *Synthesizing Gravity: Selected Prose* (New York: Grove Press, 2020).

Acknowledgments

Several of the pieces in *Jigsaw* were first published (in a slightly different form) as the chapbook *Some of the Puzzles* (Ottawa: above/ground press, July 2021), with thanks to editor rob mclennan.

"Notes on the Biscuit Puzzle" was published online by the *Walrus* (May 27, 2022), with thanks to editors Jessica Johnson and Monika Warzecha.

My continued deep thanks to Kevin Williams and the Talon team for supporting my work and, in particular, to editor Catriona Strang for her wise guidance and humour, andrea bennett for their amazing line drawings, and Leslie Smith for the book's cover and interior design.

Thank you, once again, to my long-time editor, Karl Siegler, for his help in re-visioning the text.

Love and thanks to Vicky Husband, Patrick Pothier, Susan Kerr, Phil Murty, and, as ever, fellow cow enthusiast Terry Farrant.

M.A.C. Farrant is the award-winning author of eighteen works of fiction, non-fiction, and memoir, and two plays.

She has published nine books with Talonbooks, including her trio of miniature fiction, *The World Afloat* (2014), *The Days* (2014), and *The Great Happiness* (2019). Her most recent book, *One Good Thing: A Living Memoir*, was a BC bestseller.

She lives in North Saanich, British Columbia.